Praise for *The Madoffs*

"**The Madoffs Among Us** courageously tackles the untold story in professional relationships: investors beware of schemers, scammers, and over promisers. In his conversational style, Bill combines his 30 years as an honest broker with his recent and shocking study of people losing money to confidently take readers under his wing. He lands on the insidious tactics of bad apples or the Madoffs among us. Then he equips investors with the tools and financial concepts to be knowledgeable partners in their own affairs. Well-intentioned financial professionals and seasoned and novice investors will find this book fascinating."

—Gerri Leder, president, LederMark
Communications & Coaching

"Relying on Bill's long experience in the industry, he has written an easy to read and informative book that I recommend to investors and their advisors. This book provides effective steps that all investors should utilize to ensure that they are working with an honest, caring and effective financial professional."

—Timothy Scheve, president and CEO,
Janney Montgomery Scott

"This book is a wonderful read and highly informative. The author has done a great job of helping people keep those wayward and dangerous emotions in check when making financial decisions."

—Kathleen Hebbeler, PhD, behavioral research psychologist

"In Bill's book he encourages the investor to be alert, take an active role in decisions and supplies easy to understand financial concepts. I especially enjoyed the comfortable way he alerts the investor to fraud. This is a message that must be broadcast and repeated to all investors and investment professionals."

—James W. Brinkley, former president and CEO,
Legg Mason Wood Walker, Inc.

"Imagine explaining to the board of directors, staff, and clients of your nonprofit their reserves or endowment have disappeared. Anyone with experience in raising resources for nonprofits can testify to the hard work and perseverance needed to cultivate and properly steward resources. Bill has vast experience as a compassionate and diligent nonprofit volunteer leader who understands not-for-profit entities are not immune to the Madoffs among us. Bill's book should be a recommended read for all executive directors and a prerequisite for board leadership at all levels. Bill's life of servant leadership makes him the perfect person to deliver this message."

—Steven S. Kast (34 years in non-profit), president and CEO, United Way of the Virginia Peninsula

"There is a lot of experience and wisdom wrapped up in these pages. As I read it I couldn't help but think of a related Warren Buffett quote: 'When you sit down at a poker table and you don't know who the patsy is, you are the patsy.' Take the time to know whom you are dealing with. Bill's work will allow you to proceed financially with greater clarity and confidence."

—Michael Whittaker, former senior vice president, TCW Investment Management

"Bill Francavilla's new book is concurrently an easy read, and a comprehensive one. It could stand simply as a rock-solid primer on money management and investing. However, it's so much more that that! In my 40 years of policing, I've encountered too many victims of crimes, many of which are aptly described in Bill's book. The reader will be able to avoid most of the risks from scam and fraud artists when armed with Bill's advice and can eschew "too good to be true" opportunities by easily recognizing them through the many examples given. It costs far less to avoid being a victim than to recover from being a victim, and this book is a great inoculation against fraud and deliberate financial mismanagement."

—Richard W. Myers, executive director, Major Cities Police Chiefs Association

THE
MADOFFS
AMONG US

COMBAT THE SCAMMERS, CON ARTISTS, AND THIEVES WHO ARE PLOTTING TO STEAL YOUR MONEY

WILLIAM M. FRANCAVILLA, CFP®

CAREER
PRESS

The Career Press, Inc.

This edition first published in 2018 by Career Press,
an imprint of Red Wheel/Weiser, LLC

With offices at:
65 Parker Street, Suite 7
Newburyport, MA 01950
www.redwheelweiser.com
www.careerpress.com

Copyright © 2018 by William M. Francavilla, CFP®

ISBN: 973-1-63265-128-0

Library of Congress Cataloging-in-Publication Data

Library of Congress Control Number: 2018932271

Cover design by Howard Grossman/12E Design
Interior by PerfecType, Nashville, Tennessee
Typeset in ITC Berkeley Oldstyle and Bodoni MT Standard
Printed in Canada
MAR

10   9   8   7   6   5   4   3   2   1

"Now the serpent was more subtle
than any beast of the field."
Genesis 3:1

DEDICATION

To James W. Brinkley, former president and CEO, Legg Mason Wood Walker, Inc., and Raymond A. (Chip) Mason, former chairman and CEO, Legg Mason, Inc., former chairman of the Securities Industry Association.

In 1986 I had the good fortune to be hired by the Baltimore-based company Legg Mason. Legg Mason always enjoyed a wonderful reputation on the street because of the corporate culture of always putting our clients first. Our advisors and indeed all employees were constantly admonished to be honest, caring, and loving (yes, loving!). Chip Mason, Legg Mason's CEO, was fond of saying, "I don't want to see any chalk on your shoes," referring to keeping your game in the middle of the field and never too close to being out of bounds. And president Jim Brinkley had the audacity to tell us to "love" our clients.

There are many other securities industry titans who endeavored to be the best and to do the best for their clients. Jim Wheat of Wheat Securities, John Templeton of the Templeton Funds, Edward Jones, A. G. Edwards, and too many more to mention. But the two I had the pleasure to know, trust, and work for were Chip and Jim. Generations of financial advisors and clients are greatly benefited as a result of honest efforts by honest people. Their legacies continue to this day.

The overwhelming percentage of financial advisors are honest men and women acting in accordance with the "Prudent Man Rule," coined in 1830 by Samuel Putnam, which states, "Those with responsibility to invest money for others should act with prudence, discretion, intelligence, and regard for the safety of capital as well as income." And this important work is dedicated to each of them as well.

It is the knave who selfishly decides to put his or her needs above the client's and in doing so harms the person financially, sometimes irreparably. So to the Madoffs among us, look out. I'm about to turn the light on.

CONTENTS

FOREWORD

The selection of a personal financial advisor is a high priority for an investor. The risks and rewards can have a strong influence on their financial security, longevity plans, and ability to take care of themselves and share with their families and others.

The great majority of advisors are honest and work in the clients' best interest. There are a few who take shortcuts at the investors' expense. The few bad ones embarrass their profession and provide great harm to innocent investors. There is never a place for them in any industry, but they have been and will continue to prey on the innocent. Bill Francavilla has provided a blueprint for selecting an advisor most suitable to the investor. He provides the warning signs for identifying those advisors who should be avoided. Reading and understanding *The Madoffs Among Us* could become an investor's most important decision.

I've known Bill Francavilla for more than thirty years. He joined Legg Mason in 1986 with a desire to make a positive difference in the lives of his clients and their families. Bill's professional purpose was to place his clients' interest

first and help them do what they would not do without
him.

Bill was recognized for his acute understanding of
investors, which he willingly shared with other advisors.
This strong professional commitment and his communication skills led to Bill's promotion to branch manager. His
influence and basic beliefs of clients' interests first; do the
right thing; provide discovery of client needs, risks, and
goals; and deliver investment excellence led to his position
as director of wealth management and financial advisor
senior trainer. He developed the firm's C.A.R.E. program,
designed to focus maximum attention on the needs of clients. These roles involved training new and experienced
advisors. He insisted on being a good listener and empha-
sized that financial management is a personal matter.
Advisors were challenged to find solutions and never sell.

When selecting an advisor, one must know who to
avoid. Investors are encouraged to exercise caution and due
diligence. Ask yourself if you respect, trust, and like this
person. Will you be advantaged by them and their company? The advisor's firm should be well established and
strong financially, and possess a good reputation.

Bill is a giver. He believes that we have a responsibility to give back to our community and others in need. He
has volunteered his time as an emergency medical technician with his local fire department and once saved a man's
life by administering CPR. He has served as chairman of
The Boys & Girls Clubs of the Virginia Peninsula and fre-
quently takes mission trips with church groups to Cuba, El
Salvador, and other places.

In this book he encourages the investor to be alert
and take an active role in decisions, and supplies easy to

understand financial concepts. I especially enjoyed the comfortable way he alerts the investor to fraud. Bill understands that, at the intersection of naïveté and subtlety, there is danger, but by avoiding naïveté and ignorance as well as remaining vigilant to the people who would otherwise steal from us, the reader can confidently walk away from deals "too good to be true."

This is a message that must be broadcast and repeated to all investors and financial professionals.

James W. Brinkley
former president and CEO,
Legg Mason Wood Walker, Inc.

Subtlety and Naïveté: The Twin Towers of Deception

An elderly woman in Gatlinburg, Tennessee, while regularly attending church services befriended a man who others described as trustworthy and professional. Little did she know that her new "friend," a stockbroker, would defraud her of her life savings. The man, Dennis Boize, pleaded guilty to perpetrating fraud for more than six years, devastating more than 100 victims and misappropriating millions of dollars. Boize's victims included personal friends and several fellow church members. His victims never knew that Boize had a prior conviction for bank fraud and two for theft.

Bryan Berard, a professional hockey player, lost $3 million because his financial advisor decided to keep the money and not invest it as promised. Billy Joel lost $90 million because he trusted his brother-in-law. Robert De Niro lost $1 million in artwork when his art broker kept the sales money.

When I first entered the world of financial services, I knew that there were some bad guys out there who were intent on stealing money from others. I did not know, however, that some of these people were friends and classmates of mine. And thirty years later I am compelled to tell all about the depth of deception that exists not only in the world of financial services but in several other industries, such as charities, health care, IRS scams, grandparent frauds, and even romance. From my findings I have deduced that consumers need to be ever vigilant. I hesitate to say ever suspicious, but let's just say I encourage the reader to have a healthy dose of wide-eyed objectivity.

Do the names Madoff, Ebbers, Lay, and of course, Ponzi offer the reader any pause?

The subtle deceit of the ill intended, our first tower of deception, is ever present. His or her hunting ground is the world's population, and in particular the less informed.

The unsuspecting naïveté among people, most common in times of personal need and greed, completes the twin towers of deception. This is exactly when wealth is extracted by the robber barons. It has happened ever since Eve and her accomplice, Adam, fell prey to the subtlety of the serpent, and this sleight of reason will continue to occur as long as man is tempted. History suggests that this confluence between subtlety and naïveté has taken place thousands if not millions of times, and its legacy continues to this day. Shouldn't we have learned from our previous errant ways? Shouldn't thousands of years of growth and maturity have ripened us to remain alert to the many schemes that surround us and would rob us of our wealth and dignity? What is it in the human psyche that compels us to repeat the sins of our fathers? Why must we so easily and so consistently fall prey to subtlety? And because by nature, emotion governs so much of our decision-making abilities, are we susceptible beyond our control?

In 1986 I began my career in financial services as a trainee for Legg Mason, a well-respected securities firm based in Baltimore, Maryland. My class of trainees included twelve people from a variety of previous careers. Firms like Legg Mason prefer to hire men and women who have an established record of success, so most of my classmates were in their midthirties to midforties.

I recall an attorney, a schoolteacher, a medical device salesperson, and several others in my class. I had been self-employed and found a fascination with all things financial. I felt that I had found the most reputable firm I could and was very proud of being hired. There were eleven men and one woman in my class. I sat next to the woman and was certain that she would be successful. Engaging, articulate, and charming, everyone liked Monica. And her professional prowess proved me correct. Month after month Monica was either at the top of our class in revenue and new assets (measurements of success in the financial services industry) or very close to the top. She was a go-getter.

Several years later I learned that Monica was leaving Legg Mason and was opening her own brokerage firm. What I didn't know was her method of financing such a lofty venture. She turned to her clients and, according to court records, "guaranteed" them annual returns of 30 percent if they gave her their investable assets.

Mary was just such an investor. She was sixty-seven, a cancer survivor, and a widow living on a fixed income. She gave Monica, her trusted advisor, more than $100,000. "Monica promised me a future," said Mary. Monica was always affectionate with Mary, comparing her to her own mother. Mary said, "Now I have nothing, and it hurts." Mary lost her entire investment, and Monica was charged and later convicted of selling unregistered investments and guaranteeing above-market returns to potential investors like Mary.

Monica was sentenced to fifteen years in prison with all but three years suspended. At the time of sentencing, Mary told reporters, "Maybe now she's going to feel the pain we're used to feeling." Monica? The engaging, articulate, charming young lady I sat next to in training? How did this happen? How could we all have been so wrong in our opinions of her? And how did so many people believe that her manner of making them above-average returns was legitimate?

I intend to establish that any and all decisions related to investing require maximum participation on the behalf of the investor. The world of finance may seem confusing to the majority of people; nonetheless it is the men and women who entrust their hard-earned cash to others who have the most to lose. It thus becomes incumbent upon individuals to conduct their own due diligence to make certain they understand not only the promise of appreciation, income, or tax advantage but also the many ways any investment could go wrong. I intend this book to be a self-help discussion and provide the reader with actionable items throughout the composition. A critical distinction in this work is my consistency to educate the reader ever so gently. I say "gently" because I have come to understand that a relatively large segment of the population does not understand or chooses not to understand the many nuances of finances. Armed with a cursory understanding of the industry jargon and equipped with critical questions, even the most novice among us are better prepared to hold on to their wealth.

The world of investing is indeed daunting, but also very exciting, and many people have enjoyed the benefits of wise decisions in the marketplace. But there are land mines, and one's ability to navigate around these mines is critical. I am an absolute proponent of participating in the securities markets. I love it. I watch the futures each morning and am a voracious reader of current market opinions and trends. I have a list of favorite money managers who speak the truth as they see it—some directly at odds with each other but all presenting compelling cases as to why they're right.

Who do we believe? Can we discern the good ideas from the bad, or must our emotions always get in the way? How can investors minimize the chances of losing money at the hands of the Madoffs among us? In addition to investment scams, let's visit the most notorious and popular "too good to be true" offers from home repairs to romance. How do we discern the honest from the dishonest? In subsequent chapters you will find the questions you must ask of your financial advisor, the three types of financial individuals that should probably be avoided, the terms and concepts that you must understand before engaging an advisor, and a general review of terminology used by employees in the financial industry.

The reader will learn to recognize the dangerous intersection where the subtlety of the perpetrator and the naïveté of the consumer meet. Money is lost when the twin towers of deception—subtlety and naïveté—collide. My hope is that when one reaches this intersection, they simply stop, enjoy an a-ha moment, and thank me for warning them.

CHAPTER 1

PAY ATTENTION
OR PAY DEARLY

"I've had a wonderful time, but this wasn't it."
—Groucho Marx

NHL great Bryan Berard is my new hero. Most people who are defrauded or scammed out of their savings either don't want to admit it or are too embarrassed to tell. Not Bryan. He lost about $3 million to a purported investment professional he met through a mutual friend. While Bryan was busy making money playing hockey, Phil Kenner was busy spending it. Kenner told Berard that he was making Hawaiian real estate purchases that would grow exponentially in value. Kenner had also defrauded a number of other NHL players as he became the broker to the pros. ·

According to Berard, "I was playing in Russia in 2009, and I started paying more attention, which I probably should have been doing earlier in my career, but I started paying attention to a lot of deals to do with Kenner and things weren't matching up."[1]

Kenner and an accomplice, Tommy Constantine, were eventually convicted of wire fraud, wire-fraud conspiracy, and money-laundering conspiracy. Kenner and Constantine knew as much about playing hockey as Berard and several other professionals know about personal finances. "He [Kenner] knew when guys were playing hockey, we were concentrating on hockey," said Berard.[2]

Kelly Currie, acting United States Attorney for the Eastern District of New York, is quoted as saying, "Driven by personal greed, Kenner and Constantine spent years lying to investors and stealing their money, and then attempted to conceal their fraud by repeatedly and brazenly avoiding responsibility, shifting blame and scapegoating others."[3]

As impressive as Bryan Berard was on the ice, with 76 goals and 247 assists in 619 career games, what impresses me most are his courage, honesty, and resolve to warn other professional athletes about bad people who steal their wealth. If this were an isolated case of a pro athlete or public person getting scammed, we would all agree how unfortunate this was for the victim. But this is one of thousands of similar cases where people earn money plying their trade only for the funds to be absconded by bad guys.

In 2012, the Certified Planner Board of Standards conducted the Senior Financial Exploitation Study. The study revealed the following:

- 74% of investors may have purchased unsuitable products.
- 58% of advisors omitted important facts.
- 48% may have misrepresented an investment.
- 46% are guilty of negligence or lack of follow-up.
- 19% committed fraud with intent or lying.[4]

It's actually the last point, indicting 19 percent of advisors, that concerns me most. I'm going to chalk up the previous (albeit alarming) findings to human behavior. Yes, financial advisors are human and might omit a fact or not follow up properly but to outright defraud? Unacceptable.

The information in this book, when utilized in conversations with advisors, will greatly minimize the probability of fraudulent activity. But it's not foolproof. Look at the following examples of people who should have known better or maybe were better equipped to uncover fraud because they have the advantage of attorneys and accountants presumably assisting their financial efforts.

How about Billy Joel, who lost $90 million? His wife Elizabeth's brother, Frank Weber, godfather to Joel's daughter, became his financial manager. Weber enriched himself at Billy Joel's expense by funding several of his own businesses, taking unauthorized loans. Weber also double-billed Joel for services rendered. Worst of all, he fabricated financial statements and convinced his client, Joel, that they were doing quite well. Readers will ask themselves, "How in the world did someone steal $90 million? Didn't someone as smart as Billy Joel suspect something was wrong?"

After several years, Billy Joel hired an attorney and accounting firm to do an investigative audit of his financial

position. This effort resulted in the uncovering of one of
the largest scams perpetrated upon any one individual. Joel
trusted Frank Weber. Naturally one would trust a family
member, especially one who probably swooned over one's
baby girl. Weber knew the trust was high, and he also
knew that this brilliant songwriter and performer probably
knew very little about investments and finance. Subtlety
and naïveté were able to rear their ugly heads and cause
major financial mayhem. It wasn't until Joel introduced
objectivity, experience, and expertise to the equation that
naïveté gave way to truth. In retrospect, Billy Joel probably wishes that he had enlisted the support of his attorney and accountant much sooner as doing so would have
saved him a fortune, but we are human, subject to human
frailties and emotions. Like you and me, he chose to trust
the subtle Frank Weber; after all, his specialty was earning
millions of dollars, not investing it. Billy Joel was in the
same position as all people who are conned, scammed, and
defrauded. He was caught at the intersection of subtlety
and naïveté. Billy Joel was very busy doing what he did
best, composing and singing.[5]

Robert De Niro became ensnared with a crooked art
collector named Lawrence Salander. Salander stole more
than $88 million from investors and art owners. This list
included such notables as Robert De Niro and tennis professional John McEnroe. It seems Salander sold fifty pieces
of artwork belonging to De Niro for a huge profit and
kept the money to pay off his own debts. De Niro's father,
Robert Sr., was the artist, and his son was very proud of
his father's achievements; Robert Jr. would showcase his
father's artwork around the world. He and so many others
never imagined that Salander, a highly reputed art dealer,

would ever betray them. Salander, currently serving time at a medium-security prison in New York, enjoyed a lavish lifestyle, one that he could hardly afford. So he simply stole art and sold it for his own profit. He finally pleaded guilty to thirty counts of grand larceny and fraud, having stolen more than $100 million of artwork. In a *Barron's* article, author Philip Boroff states, "There are lessons galore here, from the dangers of doing deals with 'friends' in a murky business you don't really understand, to the ease with which art dealers who have been to jail continue to practice their trade."[6] Sounds like so many victims of Lawrence Salander found themselves at the same intersection as Billy Joel. "Pay attention or pay dearly" is more than just a catchy phrase. It is real, and real consequences follow anyone unfortunate enough to wade into an arrangement where subtlety and naïveté pervade.

Gordon Matthew Thomas Sumner (aka Sting) lost $9.8 million to his advisor of fifteen years, Keith Moore. Moore took the funds and invested them on various deals, including a chain of Indian restaurants in Australia, a scheme to convert Russian military aircraft into passenger planes, and development of an ecologically friendly gearbox. With the balance, Moore paid off his considerable debt. Sting claimed that his personal financial system, designed by Moore, involved 108 accounts and was hard to "get a handle on." Sting simply didn't have the time to pore over his investments, as he too was busy earning the money, not investing it. Interestingly enough, Moore had previously declared bankruptcy and had been disciplined three times for professional misconduct after clients levied complaints against him.[7]

According to a study conducted by Mark Egan, Gregor Matvos, and Amit Seru entitled "The Market for Financial Advisor Misconduct," dated February 29, 2016, between the years 2005 and 2015 over 45,000 advisors were disciplined for misconduct.[8] That figure works out to be 7 percent of the advisor population. What is especially alarming is that if the advisor was indeed terminated for his or her discretions, 44 percent were back working at another financial firm within one year. Is it any wonder why the Edelman Trust Barometer 2015 ranked financial advisors among the least trustworthy professionals in America?[9] When one considers that over 650,000 advisors help manage more than $30 trillion and that 56 percent of Americans seek professional advisors, we better well be vigilant.

There are not hundreds of examples of people being defrauded. There are hundreds of thousands of ordinary Americans being conned and scammed each and every year. It's not only professional athletes and performers who are too busy earning lots of money to pay attention. It's you and me as well. Most Americans outside the financial industry are busy earning income and taking care of their families. They hire trusted advisors to help them grow their assets in the hope of retiring comfortably, bequeathing assets to heirs or charities, or simply funding education for children. Their business may be medicine, education, civil service, military, and many other disciplines. They don't have the time, interest, or expertise to engage in the day-to-day rigors of financial management. It is incumbent upon each and every person to be vigilant and participate to the extent they can in the financial process.

So are there constants? Are there warning signs? Are there measures that we can take to minimize the probability of being scammed? The answer is an unequivocal and resounding *yes*. But notice that I said "minimize the probability." This was quite deliberate because mine is not a foolproof system, and I don't believe one exists. This is merely an attempt to equip you, the consumer and investor, with tools to fortify and protect your wealth. Some of the individuals I will describe made the national headlines (similar to the aforementioned) and others were what I call the Madoffs next door. These are the truly sinister, as they prey upon the moms and pops of the world and take delight in spending other people's money.

The constants include the two pillars of deception: naïveté and subtlety. Trusting men and women like Berard, De Niro, Sting, Joel, and millions of others simply believe that the people who promise to deliver safety and high returns are noble, intelligent professionals. In reality, the bad people are often subtle financial sociopaths who feel no remorse while stealing the savings of so many, thus ruining their financial lives. Rather, they delight in their abilities to deceive people and feel that they (the investors) are so gullible, they deserve to lose their savings.

And we are all perfectly capable of losing money to others. Your humble author was victimized by a con game many years ago. I was convinced I was dealing with honest inventors who had a legitimate new product that would revolutionize automobile gas efficiency. Several thousand dollars later, I found out that it was a façade, and the principals of the company were convicted and imprisoned. Victims, such as me, say, "I never thought he would do such a thing." Of course—otherwise you and I would never have trusted the person in the first place.

When faced with the opportunity to buy an investment or other opportunity, we should ask ourselves the following two questions:

1. Do I know enough about this financial opportunity to make an educated and prudent decision?
2. Is this person who wants me to buy his or her opportunity too new to the business, too "salesy," or just too opinionated?

Maybe if I just ask for a referral from a friend who knows a financial advisor or has done business with him. His or her website seems to be so professional, they can't possibly be dishonest. He or she has impeccable credentials or investment history.

Permit me to remind you that the several people referenced thus far did just that. They were referred or impressed with the person whom they entrusted, and they were bitterly disappointed.

Please let me also remind you that the overwhelming majority of investment professionals are honest, caring professionals who genuinely do a stellar job for their clients. They are not sales focused, but rather solutions focused. With them reside what's great about the financial services industry. I have spent more than thirty years helping people reach their financial goals. And during my tenure many colleagues and I have made wrong decisions about investments or markets. But wrong decisions about investments are quite different from dishonest intentions. The point is, no one is impervious to market corrections or just plain bad decisions, but I'd rather make a bad deal with a good person than a good deal with a bad one. To the thousands of good advisors, I salute you and support you. You are making wonderful improvements in the lives of so many Americans as you solve their financial puzzles.

Investors should hire problem-solvers and not sales-people. When the advisor focuses on providing you with a solution to your stated problem (for example, retirement planning, funding education, making sure you are properly insured against risk, minimizing taxes, ensuring tax-advantaged bequeathing of estate assets), you're in good company. On the other hand, when you find yourself at a free luncheon or dinner at which an advisor has a single product designed to solve all your problems, or when you receive an unsolicited call from your or an unknown broker with a deal you can't ignore, watch out. Here is where you ask your two questions: Do I know enough about the investment, and do I know enough about the advisor? If you can't answer yes to both questions, step back.

In my study of people losing money, I've come to recognize that the bad guys perpetrate many services and businesses. It may be romance, charities, grandparents, or other family scams; home repair rip-off; health-care fraud; or investments. The bad guys know some things that you and I don't. They know that they can be most successful operating in an environment in which most people are inexperienced. They know charitable giving is almost always emotion driven. They know that greed and fear both sell. They know that by simply referencing something as scary as the Internal Revenue Service they've introduced fear to the inexperienced. They have become expert at using the Internet and obtaining people's Social Security numbers and credit card numbers. They know how to handle objections by giving the potential victim a sense of urgency.

("This offer will only be available until 5:00 this evening!") They are proficient at tugging at heartstrings, or appealing to one's greed and fear. They also know that their window of opportunity with any one person is limited. They may be running from town to town or state to state to keep ahead of the law. A quick sale is just that, and prudent consumers must ask themselves the aforementioned, "Do I know enough about this investment, and do I know the person trying to sell me?"

What about five of the greatest con artists in the history of the world? I call them the Infamous Five and describe their personas and crimes so as to advantage the reader. It's helpful to recall how Madoff, Ponzi, Law, Lay, and Ebbers each perpetrated their respective crimes. And perhaps by recognizing similar traits we can indeed stay one step ahead of the bad guys.

CHAPTER 2

THE INFAMOUS
FIVE

*"O, what a tangled web we weave
when we first practice to deceive."*
—Sir Walter Scott

There are probably three divisions of Bad People. I submit that they can be considered infamous, famous, and the guy next door. I took license assigning these three designations choosing to classify them relative to either the extent of their deception or their professional status.

Ancient and certainly recent history provides us with examples of thousands of financial reprobates. It is important to understand personal aspects of these individuals as well as the ploys they've perpetrated upon unsuspecting but very willing "investors."

It is also important to understand that not all bad advisors conduct so-called Ponzi schemes. But these are the people who oftentimes pull off the truly outrageous and make large sums of illegal money by paying early investors with newly acquired money from later investors. It works until the perpetrator runs out of new investors. Just as a rapidly appreciating market compels ever more investors to chase returns, it's always the low man on the totem pole who loses most. These are the people who trusted the person, the market, or the government to solve their problems—and of course they are always the people who wind up losing their money.[1]

Bernie Madoff

Bernie Madoff was born in Queens, New York, in 1938, the son of Ralph and Sylvia Madoff. His parents had married during the Depression and struggled financially for many years. In the 1950s, Ralph became involved in finance, registering as a broker-dealer for a company he started, Gibraltar Securities. (Many have suggested that the company was a front for Ralph's unethical dealings.) Ralph, however, was not successful. After he failed to report the condition of his company's finances, the SEC (Securities and Exchange Commission) forced Ralph to close his business. The couple's house also had a $13,000 tax lien that went unpaid from 1956 until 1965.

After graduating from Hofstra University in 1960, son Bernie started his own investment firm. Using $5,000 that he earned from two summer jobs, one as a lifeguard and the other installing sprinkler systems, Madoff and his wife, Ruth, established Madoff Investment Securities, LLC, the same company he would maintain and act as chairman of until his arrest in 2008. His father-in-law, an accountant, referred hundreds of people to Madoff's company. One of those referred was Carl Shapiro, an apparel executive who gave Madoff tens of thousands to initially invest. Forty years later, Madoff called on Shapiro to help him, and much to Shapiro's everlasting regret, Shapiro complied. (We will learn later that Shapiro would lose a total of $545 million.)

To compete with firms that were members of the New York Stock Exchange (NYSE), Madoff's firm began using new computer technology for client quotes. Eventually this technology helped develop the NASDAQ, the second-largest stock exchange in the world, after the NYSE. Madoff Securities succeeded by quoting both a buy and sell price with the goal of making a profit on the bid-offer spread. This is the difference between what a buyer pays for a stock and a seller receives. The *Wall Street Journal* wrote that "Mr. Madoff's firm can execute trades so quickly and cheaply that it actually pays other brokerage firms a penny a share to execute their customer's orders, profiting from the spread between bid and ask prices that stocks trade for."[2] Pretty enticing endorsement from a revered financial publication.

Madoff's was also one of the first firms to use electronic trading. In the late 1970s and early 1980s, he recognized its potential and hired people to design software that could trade stocks in seconds. Not only was this technology exceedingly efficient, it was very inexpensive. In those days, there was a prevailing spread of at least twelve cents (1/8th) between the price that a firm would pay to buy shares and the price at which it would sell the same shares. The client, of course, paid this "spread," or fee, all perfectly legal and quite traditional.

By the 1980s, Madoff Securities, LLC was handling up to 5 percent of trading on the NYSE; a decade later it would handle 9 percent.

To this point, Madoff was legitimate. As most Ponzi schemers, legitimacy is crucial, at least in the early stages of the fraud. Perhaps he never intended to defraud others and simply got caught up in a situation that could not be controlled? No one may ever know. But we can be certain that at some point Madoff knew what he was doing was terribly wrong. Did he believe that he could "undo" the damage if only he had more time or better market conditions? Madoff's crime is more recent to readers and displays so many of the ingredients necessary to extract wealth from an unsuspecting populace.

By 2000, Madoff Securities occupied three floors. Peter Madoff, Bernie's younger brother, was senior managing director and chief compliance officer. Peter's daughter, Shannon, was the compliance attorney. Mark and Andrew, Madoff's sons, worked in the trading section along with their cousin, Charles Weiner.

And then the magic happened: Word of mouth began attracting more and more investors. Bernie was skilled at marketing. His fund was considered ultra-exclusive, making it even more alluring to a certain sector of investors. He generally refused to meet directly with clients, which enhanced his aura and mystique. When asked about his stellar investment performance, clients were often told it was "too complicated" to explain. The New York Times reported that Madoff, who is Jewish, approached many prominent Jewish executives and organizations. His clientele included such famous people as Steven Spielberg, Jeffrey Katzenberg, Kevin Bacon, Kyra Sedgwick, John Malkovich, Zsa Zsa Gabor, Mortimer Zuckerman, Sandy Koufax, Larry King, World Trade Center developer Larry Silverstein, and Salomon Brothers economist Henry Kaufman.

He cleverly sold off his holdings for cash at the end of each reporting period to avoid filing disclosures of its holding with the SEC. Madoff rejected a call for an outside audit for reasons of secrecy, claiming that audits were the exclusive responsibility of his brother, Peter, the company's chief compliance officer.

To perpetrate the fraud, Madoff was shrewd enough to post steady, consistent annual returns of 10 to 12 percent. One of his funds posted annual returns of 10.5 percent for seventeen years. In 2008, the year the S&P 500 Index tanked 40 percent, the fund showed a gain of 5.6 percent.[3]

As did Carlo Ponzi a century earlier, every now and then Madoff aroused suspicion, but his various businesses were shrouded in secrecy, difficult to understand, and even harder to penetrate. The SEC investigated his securities company at least eight times over a sixteen-year period but nothing ever happened.[4] In May 2001 an article appeared in the trade publication *Mar/Hedge* that shed a light upon his investment operation, which had $6 billion to $7 billion in assets, making it the second-largest hedge fund in the world at the time. The reporter for *Mar/Hedge* was curious. How could Madoff deliver such consistent returns? Unfortunately for Madoff, a man named Harry Markopolos, a financial analyst and portfolio manager at Rampart Investment Management of Boston, observed that one of his trading partners had significant assets

with Madoff. Markopolos's bosses at Rampart asked him
to design a product that could replicate Madoff's returns.
Markopolos couldn't make the numbers add up and told
the SEC that, in his opinion, Madoff was a fraud and that it
was mathematically impossible to do what Madoff claimed.
Fortunately for Madoff, but unfortunately for his investors,
the SEC took no action.

In 2003, Renaissance Technologies, one of the most
successful hedge funds in the world, reduced its exposure to Madoff's fund first by 50 percent and eventually
completely—because of suspicions about the consistency
of returns, the fact that Madoff charged very little compared to other hedge funds, and the impossibility of the
strategy Madoff claimed to use. By 2005 his business grew
to include as much as $50 billion under management.

And then 2008 came and crushed financial markets,
largely due to subprime lending and derivative investing.
People wanted their money even though Bernie claimed
to have produced a very respectable 4.5 percent January
through October. Madoff was getting anxious and asked
his wife, Ruth, to make two transfers totaling $15.5 million
from a brokerage account to her personal bank account so
that the cash would be at hand, ostensibly to pay his investors. But the demand was far greater than $15.5 million. It
was close to $7 billion.

And what does every schemer do when pressed for
money? They go out and look for more, and that's exactly
what Madoff did. He approached Carl Shapiro, his old
friend who would lose $545 million when the scheme col-
lapsed. He also went to Fairfield Greenwich, another feeder
fund, whose cofounder on behalf of his fund invested $6
billion in Madoff's funds.

But it was too late. On the night of December 10, 2008, Madoff confessed to his sons, Andrew and Mark, who turned him in to authorities. Madoff told his sons that he had "absolutely nothing," and that "it was all just one big lie" and "basically, a giant Ponzi scheme."[5]

During his March 2009 guilty plea, Madoff admitted that there were no investments at all. He basically deposited client money into a Chase Bank account. He never invested it and certainly never generated returns such as he claimed. When a client wanted money, Madoff accessed the Chase account to pay them. On February 4, 2009, the U.S. Bankruptcy Court in Manhattan released a 162-page client list with at least 13,500 different accounts. Clients included banks, hedge funds, charities, universities, and wealthy individuals who entrusted him with more than $41 billion.

In addition to the sheer magnitude of loss, it is always the personal stories that are the most distressing. People trusted him. Suzanne Webel, a sixty-two-year-old who had been saving money for retirement for years, told the court, "Our kids are now deep in debt, we couldn't afford to pay their bills, so they had to take out huge loans, and they will have to be saddled with that for 40 years. And our retirement funds are gone."[6] Jack Cutter, who spent his whole life working as a petroleum engineer, was broke. At age seventy-nine, he had to take a job stocking shelves and working the deli counter at a local Safeway. Cutter had invested more than a million dollars with Madoff—because he trusted him. And, of course, there are countless other stories of so many who lost so much as a result of this giant swindle.

Are there similarities between Ponzi and Madoff, and the several others we will review? In a word, yes. But are

these similarities peculiar and readily observed by a trusting
individual? In another word, no.

I do believe that we can arm ourselves with knowledge and preparation. We certainly don't have to become
experts, but it is my adamant contention that by understanding some of the language of finance, some of the
strategies and yes, watching for the Ponzi/Madoff warning
signs, we can greatly reduce our exposure to this ubiqui-
tous risk. Before we investigate other notable miscreants,
let's see how Carlo and Bernie could have been fast friends.

Both were flamboyant, and certainly ambitious with a
lust for wealth. Both came from humble beginnings, were
blessed with charming personalities, and were quite generous. They also were quite independent and secretive. No
one in their inner circles, or even their family members,
had inkling as to their nefarious intent.

Now, does this mean that if I encounter an advisor
who is flamboyant, ambitious, charming, and generous he
or she is a crook? Absolutely not. I know of several men
and women who may share these attributes but are quite
honorable. Perhaps the one variable that would be suspect
is the secretive nature of one's personality that belies all
other activities. Both Ponzi and Madoff lived inside their
own self-imagined menagerie of deceit. Few people, even
closest family members and friends, knew of their illegal
intents and calculating ploys. Ruth Madoff, Bernie's wife,
told *60 Minutes* in 2012 that she had no idea of her hus-
band's business practices and was as shocked as anyone.[7]
His sons (the ones who turned him in to authorities) also
had little notion of their father's grand scheme, even though
they worked alongside him for years. Andrew Madoff, who
worked at Bernard L. Madoff Investment Securities, LLC,

with his older brother, Mark, said the first indication there was something seriously wrong with the business came on December 9, 2008, when his father asked his brother to arrange for traders' bonuses to be paid out. The following day, Andrew said he and his brother met with their parents at their apartment. Bernie then admitted to his family that he had been operating a fraud scheme. Both Andrew and Mark Madoff worked for the market-making side of the business, which was quite legitimate. Mark left the apartment and never saw his parents again, committing suicide two years later to the day of his father's arrest.

Likewise, Ponzi had hired dozens of young, early-day brokers to hawk his scheme, though not family members like Madoff. He paid them so well that no one wanted to believe, let alone hear, that this was not legitimate. Ah, subtlety. If only we were more capable of discerning truth from error. It remains one of the investor's greatest challenges.

One of the reasons—perhaps the single most important reason—that schemes work is because we, the "investors" choose to believe that "too good to be true" is really just a saying and has no merit as long as we are making money. Both Ponzi and Madoff had large numbers of ardent supporters who would reap large profits in spite of prevailing and sometimes disappointing markets.

One Madoff investor famously said "Doubt Bernie, doubt Bernie? No, you doubt God but not Bernie."[8]

Charles Ponzi

Ponzi famously proclaimed, "I landed in this country with $2.50 in cash and $1 million in hopes, and those hopes never left me."[9] No discussion of financial deception would be complete without a review of the "king" of Ponzi schemes, Carlo Ponzi himself.

Before Charles Ponzi conceived his infamous plan to defraud others, he had been twice convicted, once for forging bad checks and a second time for trying to smuggle Italian immigrants across the border into the United States. Carlo Pietro Giovanni Tebaldo Ponzi was born March 3, 1882, in Lugo, Italy. Little is known of his early years, but he would tell people he was from a wealthy family in Parma. At age 21 he arrived in Boston aboard the *S.S. Vancouver*. Carlo, as he was known, quickly learned English and took several rudimentary jobs in Boston or another city on the East Coast, usually in restaurants. As a dishwasher in one establishment, he would often sleep on the floor of the kitchen as he had little or no financial resources. He eventually was promoted to waiter but was fired after he was caught shortchanging his customers and stealing from the restaurant.

His travels took him to Montreal, where he landed a job as a teller with Banco Zarossi, a bank started by Luigi "Louis" Zarossi. Zarossi wanted to serve the influx of Italians to Canada and paid competitive rates to these immigrants. Unfortunately, he paid interest due with the more recently acquired deposits and not with bank profits, as should have been the case. Perhaps this is where Ponzi found out just how profitable this scam could be. He was a branch manager when Zarossi pulled the plug and moved to Mexico with an undetermined but reportedly large sum of the bank's money. He also left his wife and children in Canada, apparently preferring the comfort of cash.

One day, Ponzi walked into a former Banco Zarossi customer's facility, Canadian Warehousing, found the place empty, noticed a checkbook, and simply wrote himself a check for $423.58, forging the signature of one of the company's directors, Damien Fournier, who no doubt took exception to the matter. Ponzi would spend three years behind bars at St. Vincent-de-Paul near Montreal. Upon his release in 1911 he came back to the United States and got involved trying to smuggle illegal Italian immigrants into the country. He was caught and spent two years in Atlanta Prison, where he became a translator for the warden, who was trying to understand letters coming from a mobster named Ignazio "the Wolf" Lupo.

One of Ponzi's fellow prisoners, Charles W. Morse, a wealthy Wall Street businessman, became somewhat of a role model for Ponzi. It seems that Morse would feign illness by eating soap shavings, thereby "poisoning" himself and fooling prison doctors, who determined he should be released. Upon reentry to society, Ponzi made his way back to Boston, married Rose Maria Gnecco, and went to work in her father's grocery store. Never enough for Mr. Ponzi, he started an advertising business that promised business owners wide exposure. It too failed, but during the course of his business, he received a letter from a Spanish company asking about his advertising catalog. Inside the envelope was an international reply coupon (IRC.) The purpose of the postal reply coupon was to allow someone in one country to send it to a person in another country who could use it to pay the response postage.

This intrigued Ponzi, and he seized upon the idea that he could generate a profit by taking advantage of price discrepancy. IRCs were priced in the country of purchase and redeemed where stamps might be purchased less expensively. It was the perfect arbitrage and perfectly legal. (Arbitrage takes place when there is a price discrepancy of a commodity and the investor makes money by buying low and selling high, usually on another market or, in this case, another country.) So far, Ponzi was acting in a legal enterprise. It should be noted, though, that young Carlo had a flair not only for illegal enterprise but also had a mind for opportunity, and these two variables will often be a dangerous combination.

Then he got greedy. He borrowed money from friends and anyone who would listen, and sent it back to relatives in Italy. He merely asked them to purchase the postal reply coupons and mail them back to America. However, he was stymied by a huge pushback of red tape and was unable to follow through with his scheme. So he again went to his friends in Boston and borrowed more money, promising even greater returns. The early lenders were indeed making double their money. Some would receive $750 interest on a loan of $1,250. Of course, they were receiving money from the second and subsequent generations of new "investors."

Ponzi was gaining notoriety and a favorable reputation. He was hiring agents to leverage his sales and paying them handsome commissions. In February 1920 he made $5,000 (more than $63,000 in today's dollars). One month later he made another $30,000. In May the take exceeded $420,000 (more than $4.5 million in today's dollars).

Ponzi did what most nouveau riche do: He bought a mansion, one that had air conditioning (we're talking 1920). He bought his mother a first-class ticket to America on an ocean liner. He later pledged $100,000 to the Italian Children's Home in Jamaica Plain, Massachusetts, in his (by then) deceased mother's name.

As is the case with all schemers, the plot eventually unfolds. A humble Boston furniture dealer who had sold

Ponzi some furniture and didn't receive any money sued for money owed. Unfortunately for the furniture dealer, Joseph Daniels, the lawsuit was not successful. But it did start to raise the obvious questions and doubts about how a penniless immigrant could amass such a fortune in such a short period of time and not pay his bills. There was even a run on his company, Securities Exchange Company, with people demanding their money. Ponzi cleverly repaid the first to lay claim to funds, thus assuaging others. The *Boston Post* even printed a positive article about him and that resulted in investors coming out at a much, much faster pace.[10] Ponzi was making $250,000 per day. The day after the *Post*'s article Ponzi arrived at his office and was amazed at what he saw: literally thousands of people waiting, begging him to take their money. Greed on behalf of investors always exacerbates the proclivity for fraud. People abandon reason and embrace emotion.

By this time his antics alarmed officials and the Commonwealth of Massachusetts began an investigation. At about the same time two men from the *Post* were writing investigative news articles wondering just how, in a period when prevailing bank rates were 5 percent, Ponzi was able to provide ten times that in a very short period. Too good to be true?

One observer, Clarence Barron, the publisher of one of the nation's leading financial publications, noticed that Mr. Ponzi did not have even one penny invested in his own company. Concerned, Ponzi hired a publicity agent named William McMasters to spruce up his public image. Unfortunately for Ponzi, McMasters was a legitimate businessman who came upon several pieces of evidence that proved that Ponzi was indeed a con artist robbing Peter to

pay Paul. McMasters wrote a scathing article that would be
the beginning of the end for Ponzi. This all took place in
July 1920. On August 11, the *Post* published a front-page
article that proved unequivocally that there was nothing
more than "air" supporting the bubble and that Ponzi was
hopelessly insolvent.[11]

His investors, the maddening crowds that couldn't wait
to buy his IRCs for the promise of unrealistic returns, lost
practically everything invested. They received less than
thirty cents to the dollar. His investors lost approximately
$20 million ($255,500,000 in 2017 dollars). But Ponzi
had championed the dangerous quagmire of subtlety and
naïveté, and forever won a place in the annals of financial corruption and debauchery, lending his name to many
other so-called get-rich-quick schemes. He would spend 10
years in prison. Ponzi's last recorded words, as told during
one of his last interviews by reporters, were "Even if they
never got anything for it, it was cheap at that price. Without
malice aforethought I had given them the best show that
was ever staged in their territory since the landing of the
Pilgrims! It was easily worth fifteen million bucks to watch
me put the thing over."[12]

I have seen this persona up close and personal, not just
with the aforementioned young classmate of mine, but with
others who are not necessarily trying to replicate the classic
Ponzi scheme. These people are advertently or inadvertently
directing clients' funds to serve their own benefit. This may
come in the form of selling a product with a larger commission not because it is in the *client's* best interest but rather
the interest of the broker or advisor. Now, these individuals
are the absolute exception. I remember well the president of
Legg Mason Wood Walker, Jim Brinkley, an early mentor

and later friend telling his advisors over and over throughout the years, "You must care for your client's money more than they do." And fortunately, so many of us do.

So, are there certain attributes or personality flaws that are obvious and should alert the investor that this individual should be avoided? If we consider Carlo Ponzi, I posit that perhaps we can draw conclusions that are consistent with several of the individuals we will explore. Ponzi was ambitious. He wanted to be a millionaire. He was charming. Even when people were lined up outside his business demanding their money, he was cheerful, passing out donuts and coffee. He was so charming that most of the remaining crowd were convinced that he was a good guy.

John Law

Just to remind the reader that scams are nothing new, let's visit the antics of an eighteenth-century conman named John Law. He may not be as famous as Madoff and Ponzi, but this Scotsman pulled off quite a fiasco in 1700s France. And just to remind the reader that scams predate both Bernie and Carlo, permit me to introduce you to a reprobate who shares many of the personality traits of his twentieth-century brethren.

After the many wars waged by King Louis XIV, France was broke and defaulting on the debts it incurred from the war. The value of gold and silver rose and fell dramatically. The country decided to enlist the help of John Law (who had previously escaped to Holland and then to France after he killed a man in a sword fight). Law was also an economic theorist and friend of a high official in the French government. Law was a gambler and a brilliant mental calculator, known to win card games by mentally calculating the odds. He originated such economic concepts as the scarcity theory of value. His views held that the creation of money would stimulate the economy and that paper money (fiat currency) is preferred over gold or silver. He also felt that metal currency should be banned because "it paid no dividend."[13]

He was purported to be charming and persuasive. How else could a murderer of meager means ally himself with high-ranking officials?

Believing that the fluctuations were causing the problem, he established a bank with the authority to issue paper money notes to circulate cash within the economy. The bank took deposits in gold and silver, issued loans and withdrawals in paper currency, and built up reserves through the issuing of government bills and stock. Things were initially going so well that Law decided to expand. He established the Compagnie d'Occident (Company of the West), to which the French government gave control of trade between France and its Louisiana and Canadian colonies. The Louisiana Colony was vast, stretching from the Great Lakes to the Gulf of Mexico and Mississippi Gulf Coast. This gave rise to the Company of the West's more popular name, the Mississippi Company.

Financing the Mississippi Company operations was simple: Law raised money by selling shares in the company. The low interest rate on the bonds helped the French economy and ensured a more secure cash flow to the company. His successes in helping the ailing French economy heralded him as the maestro of his age, a former-day Alan Greenspan. He was widely sought after in French society and political establishment. And, he was charming!

The Mississippi Company, it turned out, was just a smaller part of a much grander empire. The company acquired the monopoly in tobacco trading with Africa and then into China and the East Indies. Law controlled virtually all trade with France and the rest of the world outside of Europe.

Law paid for these activities by issuing additional shares in the company, which could be paid with bank notes (from his bank, of course) or with government debt. Share value in the Mississippi Company skyrocketed as Law's empire expanded. Shares in the Mississippi Company started around 500 *livres tournois* (the French unit of account at the time) per share in January 1719. By December of the same year, share prices had reached 10,000 livres, an increase of 1,900 percent. Investors—or should I say speculators?—from across France and Europe, anxious to ignore "too good to be true," flocked to buy shares and participate in the "new economy." Thus, the Mississippi Bubble was forming—just waiting to burst.

As usual with financial schemes, Law overreached; he issued too many bank notes to fund purchases of shares in his company. Stock prices began falling in January 1720 as investors sold paper shares to turn profits into gold. To stop the sell-off, Law restricted any payment in gold unless it was more than 100 livres and encouraged people to accept paper notes rather than gold. The bank then promised to exchange its notes for shares in the company at the going market price of 10,000 livres. Turning stock shares into cash at this magnitude resulted in serious inflation. By January 1720, inflation, specifically for food, reached a rate of 60 percent. By September 1720 the price of a share had fallen to 2,000 livres, and by December, 1,000 livres.

The Mississippi Bubble had burst. John Law was no longer the toast of Paris. His scheme of fabricating wealth coupled with the frenzied anticipation of fabulous wealth by so many people catapulted the French economy into a disaster.

As I studied John Law and the circumstances surrounding his caper, I asked myself: Is it me, or were his antics the same as we are witnessing in present-day America? Paper money replacing gold-based currency; the unsustainable $20 trillion debt brought on by a century of wars; national banks with unlimited and relatively unregulated authority. Thomas Jefferson admonished us in the same century as John Law: "I believe that banking institutions are more dangerous to our liberties than standing armies."[14] As of the date of this writing, it remains to be seen.

Law fled to Brussels and then to Italy, where he continued to gamble and died impoverished in 1729.

Kenneth Lay

Born in a small Missouri town in 1942, Kenneth Lay grew up delivering newspapers and mowing lawns. His father was a Baptist preacher and occasional tractor salesman. Lay studied economics at the University of Missouri, from which he eventually earned a PhD. After serving in the Navy, he went to work for Humble Oil & Refining, the predecessor company to Exxon. He also worked for the Federal Power Commission and served as undersecretary for the U.S. Department of Interior.

After a succession of positions, Lay moved to Texas in 1984 to serve as chairman and CEO at Houston National Gas Co. In the freewheeling 1980s, companies were bought, were sold, and merged at a furious pace. An Omaha-based company, InterNorth, bought Houston National Gas in 1985. Lay took full advantage of the larger and more financially secure InterNorth to build up his new company, which was now called Enron. As CEO and chairman, he led the company's meteoric rise from a conservative natural gas pipeline company to an energy and trading conglomerate that was in the top ten on the Fortune 500 in 2000 and had $101 billion in alleged annual revenues.

With lavish offices that reflected its CEO's lifestyle, Enron was considered one of the "America's Most Innovative Companies" and was praised for its long-term pensions and effective management.[15] Lay was considered one of Houston's most influential power brokers, and he was a generous contributor to the Republican Party. President George W. Bush was fond of Lay, calling him "Kenny Boy."

In the late 1990s, after the deregulation of energy, the company developed, built, and operated infrastructures around the world, many of which lost money. Unbeknownst to most of the company, Lay had been selling off huge amounts of his Enron stock, worth more than $300 million, sending its price plummeting. At the same time, he was encouraging his employees to continue to buy the stock, telling them that it would rebound soon. The real crime was the inflated value of assets and cash flow while keeping liabilities off the books.

Enron even created phony congestion on California's state power grid and then, falsely claiming to relieve it, drove prices up, costing consumers tens of billions of dollars and increasing the company's profits. The scandal brought down one of the country's most venerable accounting firms, Arthur Anderson, which was effectively put out of business. The firm was supposedly auditing and reporting Enron's financials to the marketplace and obviously failed miserably.

In December 2001, Enron filed for bankruptcy. At the time, it was the largest bankruptcy filing in U.S. history. More than 20,000 employees lost their jobs, and many their life savings. Investors in the company lost billions. Lay was asked to leave (and was granted a $42.4 million compensation package).[16] In 2004, Lay was indicted for his role in the company's failure, including eleven counts of securities fraud, wire fraud, and making false and misleading statements.

Two years later, Lay was found guilty of ten counts against him. Because each count carried a maximum five-to-ten-year sentence, he could have faced up to thirty years in prison. However, Lay unexpectedly died of a heart attack during vacation in Colorado about three months before his sentencing. Enron's chief operating officer and CEO, Jeffrey Skilling, was sentenced to fourteen years in federal prison for his involvement and knowledge of the scheme.

The personal tragedies don't stop at the top. The chief officers of Enron caused the downfall, but it was the 20,000 employees and millions of Enron investors who were the real losers. Several years ago, when Enron was still a "viable" company, a friend and business associate of mine was visiting his father-in-law in Houston and was introduced to a sixty-two-year-old man who had decided to retire from Enron. My friend reviewed his statements and noticed that he had more than $6 million in his 401(k) retirement plan. It was 100 percent invested in Enron company stock. My friend, a financial advisor, warned that his concentrated position (all money invested in one stock) was exceedingly risky. The gentleman replied, "Show me an investment that can give me the same type of returns as Enron and I'll listen." Of course he could not, but still issued the sage warning. Well, within six months, the employee's retirement account was worth less than $400,000. He could not retire, and he had to seek further employment. Naïveté and subtlety reared their ugly heads once again.

Too good to be true. This unfortunate former Enron employee forgot or never knew that "trees don't grow to the sky," a common adage in the financial services business. Had he been reasonable and willing to listen to objective, time-honored counsel, he just might be enjoying a well-deserved retirement. The value of an honest, objective financial advisor cannot be underestimated.

Bernie Ebbers

Bernard Ebbers was born on August 27, 1941, in Edmonton, Alberta, Canada. He was one of five children born to a traveling salesman. He attended Mississippi College on a basketball scholarship and, upon graduation, ran a chain of hotels around the state. His career skyrocketed during the 1980s when he became involved in the telecommunication business. He proved to be quite adept at the management and acquisition of companies. In 1995 he cofounded WorldCom and was named CEO. The company bought MFS, a competitor, and two years later WorldCom acquired MCI. Ebbers earned considerable repute and wealth as a result of his rapidly growing conglomerate. As with so many nouveau riche, Bernie began to buy properties and personal interests. He bought a 500,000-acre ranch in British Columbia, a 21,000-acre farm in Louisiana, 540 acres of timberland in the South, and a minor league hockey team.

His net worth was an estimated $1.4 billion. He was able to purchase many of these acquisitions because of his equity holdings in WorldCom stock. As the stock price declined, the WorldCom board of directors authorized loans to prevent Ebbers from selling his positions in the company and further depressing the stock's price. (Shame on the board! In my opinion they were complicit. They thought they were acting in the shareholders' best interests, but in reality they were merely artificially supporting the stock price.)

Ebbers's financial world came apart in 2002 when allegations of conspiracy and fraud came to light. At that time he had a single promissory note worth more than $400 million issued from the WorldCom board. In 2005 Ebbers was convicted in what would be the largest accounting scandal in U.S. history, resulting in a $180 billion loss to investors and bankruptcy of the company and leaving 20,000 people unemployed. A 2002 class-action civil lawsuit against Ebbers and other defendants resulted in a settlement worth more than $6 billion to be distributed to more than 830,000 individuals.

I could journal thousands of records of finance industry people and others swindling people out of hard-earned dollars. For instance, Charles Keating, CEO of Lincoln Savings and Loan in Phoenix, bilked the U.S. government and 23,000 investors of $3 billion. Or how about Ivan Boesky, Michael Milken, Dennis Kowslowski, Jay Gould, or Richard Whitney? Each of these individuals proves that there will always be Madoffs among us.

A very close friend of mine, a man of considerable intelligence and maturity, just recently was subject of a scam. He received a call, purportedly from the Dominican Republic. It was his grandson—or so he thought—telling Grandpa that he was put in prison overnight because the cab he had hailed was stopped and there was a small amount of illegal drugs in the trunk. My friend, a former National Security Agency senior official, was suspicious—but was also convinced his beloved grandson was in trouble and agreed to wire $1,600 to the address he was given (by an alleged U.S. embassy representative). Of course, once the funds were wired he called his grandson's cell number. Michael was safe and sound in Maryland. When the brightest among us can be scammed, aren't we all candidates?

I'm like you. I don't think I can be had. But then I read Simon Lovell, author of *How to Cheat at Everything* tell his readers: "I love it when people say they can't be conned because to me, they're already half way towards being conned."[17] Lovell spent half his life running cons and schemes bilking thousands of people of millions of dollars. He often saw people as "walking ATM machines." In his later years he paid his debt to society and wrote books about being careful with your wealth by avoiding the bad guys.

I well recall my first year in the financial securities business. It astonished me that so many people were so willing to hand over their savings to someone whom they had only recently met. And to hand it over me, someone who was relatively new to the business of investing, was further astounding. Yet they did. I was always polite, was well dressed, and could articulate an investment opportunity to the extent I'd been trained. But mind you, I had only recently gained access to the financial industry by passing the Series 7 examination following two months of study. I attended a three-week training program where I was taught a variety of investments and suitability standards, but most of the time I was trained how to sell. As previously mentioned, my firm had one of the best reputations on the street and prided itself as hiring only the best men and women it could find. We were a definite cut above. But why were people so willing to trust me, a thirty-six-year-old guy with exactly one month of experience?

During my first month as an advisor I met a woman who had $50,000 to invest. After about fifteen minutes in my office (more of a cubicle), she told me she had "complete confidence" in whatever decision I would make on her behalf. Wow! Did she know I was a virtual neophyte and I was going to invest her money based on limited experience? No, and I didn't tell her. I did, however, place the monies in a total return mutual fund with a respectable record of consistent returns. So in my mind I did her a favor, and in her mind she had "complete confidence." In retrospect, after thirty years in the business, it was indeed the right decision, and I would make the same recommendation today based on her needs and goals. *But,* I could have suggested any number of opportunities and she would still tell me she had complete confidence.

I surmised then, and am fully persuaded now, that she had complete confidence in me because she was abdicating her responsibility simply because she would rather trust than learn. Let's face it: The financial landscape can be daunting, and most people have little proclivity for mastering the nuances of investing. So, they trust! It's just easier. They choose to trust and when they are referred to someone or like someone or believe someone because they have a polite and nonthreatening demeanor, they're all in.

And therein lies the crux.

When a successful person recommended a friend invest with "my guy, Bernie" or with Charles Ponzi because he was delivering double-digit returns when the bank was only yielding 5 percent, we say, "Of course!" When the markets are racing toward new highs as they did in the late 1990s (and as they are as of this writing) we want in regardless of price/earnings multiples. When the Powerball Lotto reaches lofty heights more people take more chances than normal. The sheer excitement of momentum and the opportunity to make real money really quickly ignites the fuse of greed.

CHAPTER 3

THE MADOFFS NEXT DOOR

"He who permits himself to tell a lie once,
finds it much easier to do a second time and
a third until at length it becomes habitual."
—Thomas Jefferson

Quite candidly, it's not the Madoffs, Ponzis, Laws, Lays, or Ebberses that are the most troubling. Yes, of course, their nefarious activities bilked billions of dollars from thousands of individuals. But their notoriety and public personae betrayed their initial subtlety. The miscreants that are potentially more menacing are the ones who prey upon the far less financially astute. Whereas Madoff, for instance, had the wealth of a highly sophisticated clientele, the people I'm talking about here could probably never get away with defrauding the same people. They are just too "small" or "less significant." Nonetheless, they are financially lethal.

So in addition our "infamous five," permit me to introduce you to Michael Donnelly, Buddy Persaud, Levi David Lindeman, and several others who have taken liberties with other people's money. Their antics and ploys hopefully will serve as fair warning to all readers. But let's review other important studies that will provide further reasons as to why we all fall prey.

Each year, *ThinkAdvisor,* a publication distributed to people primarily in the financial services business, lists their so-called Dirty Dozen, a list of the twelve individuals found guilty of defrauding unsuspecting people. I chose the following people to showcase the several ways advisors can steal money. Included are people who made the 2013 and 2016 Dirty Dozen lists, but the schemes never really change from year to year. They tend to be the old tried-and-true scams that have bilked people over and over and for generations. They will continue unless more Americans guard themselves. The informed need not be victims.

Michael Donnelly

According to the U.S. Attorney's office of Eastern District Pennsylvania, on April 11, 2016, Michael Donnelly, forty-seven, of Lecanto, Florida, was sentenced to ninety-nine months in prison for an investment scheme that bilked his friends and clients of nearly $2 million. He pleaded guilty in 2015 to one count of wire fraud and one count of securities fraud. U.S. District Court Judge Edward G. Smith ordered restitution, but this seldom occurs because the advisor has spent all the money. (Bernie Madoff's victims have received only $11 billion of the $65 billion he stole as of this writing.)

Between November 2007 and August 2014, Donnelly persuaded about a dozen investors, many of whom were elderly, to allow him to invest their money in securities or certificates of deposit. But instead of investing his clients' money, Donnelly appropriated the investment funds for his own use. One particularly onerous ploy is for the advisor to fabricate statements suggesting that their account values are doing well. In one case Donnelly merely switched the name on another client's statement, one that held high-quality stocks. The victim didn't realize anything was wrong and believed the securities belonged to him.[1]

Gurudeo "Buddy" Persaud

Persaud (a derivative of the word *persuade,* which this author found interesting), somehow "persuaded" people that if they only looked to the stars they could do well in the market. No, seriously! So his firm, White Elephant Trading Co., took $1 million from investors, promising "sky high" returns. In a civil judgment entitled *Securities and Exchange Commission v. Gurudeo Persaud,* the commission alleged that, while associated with Money Concepts, Persaud started his own company and raised more than $1 million from investors while promising them 6 percent to 18 percent annual returns and a risk-free investment in White Elephant's private equity fund, which would invest in futures and other markets. Persaud made numerous misrepresentations and omissions to investors, including guaranteeing their investments were secure, and failing to disclose his trading strategies were based on lunar cycles and the gravitational pull between the Earth and the moon. In actuality, he misappropriated nearly half the investors' investments into personal use. He's now spending three years behind bars.[2]

When advisors "guarantee" returns, they have transcended the law. Returns are based on probabilities, past performance and general market conditions. To represent them in any other manner is simply a lie.

Levi Lindemann

Lindemann, forty, pleaded guilty to one count of mail fraud and one count of money laundering. According to his guilty plea, between 2009 and 2014, Lindemann owned and operated Gershwin Financial, Inc., which did business under the name Alternative Wealth Solutions (AWS). He sold annuities and insurance products as well as provided financial planning services to clients in Minnesota and Wisconsin. According to his plea, he used AWS to solicit investor funds from approximately fifty clients, encouraging them to surrender their retirement accounts so that he could invest the funds in secured notes or legitimate vehicles. Instead of investing, Lindemann used the money to pay personal expenses, convert investments to cash for his own use, purchase an Infiniti QX56 sport utility vehicle, and make Ponzi-type payments of promised returns to other investors. He created counterfeit secured notes and provided them to his clients as proof of their holdings. He received seventy-four months in prison and was ordered to pay $1.9 million in restitution.[3]

Richard A. Zakarian

Zakarian, forty-eight, a tax consultant, stole $4.4 million from charities and businesses. Oh, also churches. He simply absconded with the funds. Again, it was wire fraud and making false income tax returns that landed him in prison for seventeen-and-a-half years after he pleaded guilty.

According to court records, Zakarian was a Certified Financial Planner and tax preparer who owned and operated several business ventures. Many of the payroll tax victims were churches, charities, and other nonprofit organizations that he lured as clients through purported grants from charities he claimed to operate. "This defendant preyed on non-profits, churches and small businesses that struggled to make ends meet while making their communities better," Steven M. Dettelbach, U.S. Attorney for the Northern District of Ohio, said. "He never meant to help them, only to defraud them. This was a systemic, deliberate pattern of behavior that took place over years."[4]

A number of his clients were retired, out of work, or nearing retirement. Most invested through Zakarian by moving their money from traditional, relatively safe and dependable stocks, bonds, and mutual funds. In one case, he convinced a recently retired client to pay an early withdrawal penalty to move money from a certificate of deposit. In another, he induced the client to redeem a life insurance annuity to generate investment funds and talked her out of using the money to pay off her home mortgage or car loans.[5]

Gary H. Lane

Lane, sixty, a former financial advisor, was found guilty of taking $2.7 million from six investors. These were older investors who were persuaded to let him make investments through an e*Trade account that was outside his business practice. At the time he was an advisor with Merrill Lynch. Lane had been an advisor for over thirty years. His wife would deposit the money to the e*Trade account, and Lane would then access the account to pay for personal expenses or to satisfy other investors. He was sentenced to ten years in prison. Incidentally, Merrill Lynch did the right thing by making restitution to the investors.

The U.S. Attorney for the District of Nevada, Daniel G. Bogden, said, "Beware of persons who offer better interest rates than traditional sources. They prey on the elderly and unsophisticated and will use numerous methods to steal your money. If you do not know if an investment opportunity is legitimate, it is always better to investigate the person and company before turning over any money."[6] Bravo, counselor, well said.

James Tagliaferri

Seventy-five-year-old Tagliaferri was sentenced to six years in prison for defrauding clients by funneling money to a horse-racing firm based in New York. He also purchased thinly traded securities in exchange for financial kickbacks. Upon hearing from his former clients, U.S. District

Judge Ronnie Abrams told Tagliaferri, "You breached that trust, and you should be ashamed."[7]

In 2007 Tagliaferri began executing a scheme to defraud clients in various ways. He began taking undisclosed fees in exchange for shares in the securities of a horse-racing company located in Garden City, New York. He then placed at least $40 million of client funds in investments relating to the company as well as other companies. Tagliaferri used client funds for improper purposes, including making payments to other clients who were demanding their money and to make payments on behalf of companies with whom he was affiliated. Once those monies had transferred, he used the funds for his own purposes. Guilty of investment advisor fraud, securities fraud, and wire fraud, he caused his clients to lose millions. He invested more than $120 million for at least $3.35 million in kickbacks, and when some of his clients wanted their money back, he simply used other clients' money to repay them. One client, upon hearing the sentencing, yelled, "I hope he rots in jail!"[8]

David Williams

Williams, the former president and CEO of Morgan Peabody, pleaded guilty to wire fraud and tax charges. The fifty-four-year-old was found guilty of an investment scam resulting in sixty investors losing almost $4 million. He told investors that they were buying a real estate trust and in a sense it was: his own residence, a 6-million-dollar home in Toluca Lake, California. He also committed tax evasion by failing to report more than $2.3 million and will be required to pay $777,881 in back taxes as well as civil fraud penalty and interest. The FBI uncovered the scam, and he faces seventy years in the pokey. In a plea agreement filed with the court, Williams admitted that he directed Morgan Peabody representatives to sell securities in a fund that Williams personally had created, purportedly to invest in real estate. The Sherwood Secured Investment Fund, LLC, a Studio City, California, business that Williams owned, offered a 9 percent annual return on investment.[9]

Robert Tricarico

Until April 2015, Tricarico was a registered securities broker with the Financial Industry Regulatory Authority. He was formerly employed or associated with RNT Wealth Management, Northstar Wealth Partners, LPL Financial, and Wells Fargo Advisors Financial Network. He acted as a financial advisor for an elderly and infirm victim who had substantial assets. Tricarico misappropriated more than $1.1 million from the victim by writing numerous checks to himself or for his benefit without the victim's authorization. He also liquidated a coin collection and cashed checks made payable to the victim.

Additionally, Tricarico defrauded two other victims of $20,000 by falsely representing to them that he would use their investments for a business venture and guaranteed rate of return. He used those funds as well for his own personal use.[10]

Bryan Binkholder

"He's no Bernie Madoff," said his attorney, Albert S. Watkins. "The amounts were obviously significantly less, for one, and two, this is a man who did not take money for the purpose of enriching himself personally or driving fast cars or living a loose life with wayward women or engaging in a lavish lifestyle."[11] Huh? The judge gave Binkholder nine years in prison. The court determined that Binkholder was guilty of diverting clients' funds (no matter how seemingly small) in a "hard money lending"[12] program. Binkholder's hard money lending program included providing loans to real estate developers to flip properties for a profit. Investors lost more than $3.6 million according to the U.S. Attorney's Office.

Binkholder labeled himself "The Financial Coach" and provided investment and financial planning advice to the general public through his affiliated websites, YouTube channel, published books, and an investment-related talk-radio show that aired on local stations. True, "he's no Bernie Madoff," as his attorney proclaimed, but if you or I were a victim it wouldn't matter. As a registered representative Binkholder and all advisors are limited to representing sanctioned investments. Once an advisor strays to represent unregistered or non-traded investments, they are, in my opinion, dangerously close to violating the public trust.

Gignesh Movalia

Movalia, forty, a Tampa, Florida, investment advisor was sentenced to eighteen months in prison and ordered to pay restitution of $5.4 million for perpetrating an investment fraud scheme involving Facebook stock. In connection with his guilty plea, Movalia admitted that he used the fund to defraud investors. In 2011 and 2012, Movalia raised more than $9 million from 130 investors by falsely claiming to have access to pre–initial public offering shares of Facebook, Inc. Rather than using this money to buy Facebook shares as promised, however, Movalia invested the money in other securities and concealed that fact from investors. By September 2013, when it went into receivership, Movalia's company, OM Global Fund, lost approximately $9 million, with $6 million of those losses as a result of the fraud scheme. He had in fact lost a total of $9 million of the $14 million raised from investors.

The good news is that the regulators seek out the bad guys and prosecute. The bad news is that even though they mete out justice and punish the guilty, thousands of people lose millions of dollars.

Sean Meadows

Financial advisor Sean Meadows, forty-two, was sentenced to twenty-five years in prison after his conviction of stealing more than $13 million. Meadows admitted to swindling more than 100 people in several states. His was a years-long scheme using his financial planning firm as a cover. He purportedly convinced his victims in Minnesota, Indiana, Arizona, and elsewhere to tap their retirement and other savings accounts by promising high rates of returns, up to 10 percent.

Of course, his promises were never kept. Instead, Meadows built a classic Ponzi scheme, using money from new investors to make interest and/or principal payments to existing investors. Prosecutors added that he used his clients' money to pay expenses on personal investment properties and personal credit card bills. He made payments to his spouse, bought a vehicle, traveled to Las Vegas, gambled at casinos and online, and spent more than $100,000 on sex-oriented entertainment. "Sean Meadows pretended to be a trusted investment advisor, but he abused that trust by lying to and stealing from his clients," said Minnesota Commerce Commissioner Mike Rothman. "Instead of investing his clients' hard-earned retirement savings, he used their money to bankroll his own extravagant lifestyle. Meadows not only robbed his victims of their lifetime savings. He also robbed them of their peace of mind and their dreams of a secure retirement."[13]

Aequitas Management

Aequitas Management and its three top officers stole at least $350 million, according to the SEC. CEO Robert J. Jesenik, executive vice president Brian Oliver, and former chief financial officer M. Scott Gillis continued to solicit millions of dollars to stave off an impending collapse of the company. The three drew up and sold promissory notes at 8.5 percent while investing in the now-defunct Corinthian Colleges. One investor claimed Bob Jesenik was one of his closest friends. They golfed, went to college football games, and socialized as best of friends. "Basically, everything I had was invested there," said the 80-year-old client and "best friend." "My entire life savings, the inheritance of my four sons and the profit sharing plan of my employees . . . everything."[14] He has sold his house and gone back to work to survive.

The plaintiffs and former clients of Aequitas Management filed a lawsuit against the lawyers and accountants who worked for Aequitas, claiming they knew or should have known the Lake Oswego company was a financial train wreck that misled its hundreds of investors.[15]

=====

Unfortunately, this chapter doesn't end. I could reference hundreds more who were found guilty of similar crimes. The two constants—subtlety and naïveté—are ever present. The bad guys continue to prey using deceit and lies disguised in the form of subtle persuasion. People, even the well informed, simply want to believe because of the opportunity for huge financial gain. Remember Martin Shkreli, the thirty-four-year-old who ran MSMB Capital and MSMB Healthcare? He's the guy who raised the price of the drug Daraprim, which treats a parasitic infection from $13.50 a tablet to $750 per tablet. He was found guilty in August 2017 of three counts of fraud. The SEC, responding to Martin Shkreli's recent conviction, opined, "Shkreli's victims were sophisticated. They have sufficient knowledge and experience in financial and business matters to make them capable of evaluating the merits and risks of the prospective investment."[16] The SEC knows full well that it indeed takes two parties to consummate the crimes. Even the people who should know better apparently don't.

As a financial services professional, I read industry magazines and try to stay apprised with current events in the financial marketplace. It is a rare exception when I can read a periodical like *Investment News,* a well-respected weekly magazine, where there is no mention of fraud. Frankly, I don't think there ever has been an issue that hasn't made note of fraudulent activity by an advisor. Articles with titles such as "Ex-JP Morgan Broker Gets 5 Years" and "Advisor

Siphoned $53M: SEC" or "Brothers Charged with Ponzi Scam on Elderly" permeate the pages.

The Department of Labor and FINRA (Financial Industry Regulatory Authority) enacted new legislation in April 2016 designed to make it illegal for advisors to act in their own best interest. In other words, financial advisors are legally compelled and bound to act in the best interests of their clients. (This new law has been delayed due to pushback from the Trump administration. We shall see how this plays out between Senator Elizabeth Warren, who championed the legislation, and R. Alexander Acosta, Trump's new Labor Secretary.)

Previously, advisors were ethically encouraged to act in this appropriate manner but now it is the letter of the law with tougher penalties and sanctions. It's so unfortunate that the Feds had to enact legislation to this extent. The law of unintended consequences suggests that this will be a boon to attorneys who have more laws to interpret and prosecute. The financial services industry correctly complains that this legislation may preclude smaller investors from being served. It's just too expensive. I always thought that the vast majority of advisors don't need further review and legislation. But because of the few miscreants who take unfair advantage of others, the Department of Labor enacted the new rulings.

So what can we deduce? The overwhelming majority of advisors do a terrific job. They have always acted in their clients' best interests. They follow time-honored principles of the financial services industry and honestly determine the needs of individual clients and families, and make suitable recommendations to assist people in reaching their stated goals. And I mentioned previously that an honest relationship with a financial professional helps direct appropriate actions and helps to eliminate emotional decisions.

We can also deduce that the financial services environment has a few unscrupulous individuals who will cheat you out of your hard-earned wealth. They make all the news and the government and regulators respond by imposing more laws that drive up costs for all of us. And frankly, the unintended consequence of the new legislation may be less advice and less objective advice; we'll see. The operative resolution of the book you are reading continues to try to help you discern the good guys from the bad.

CHAPTER 4

WHY SO MANY PEOPLE FALL PREY

"I love it when people say they can't be conned because to me they're already half way to being conned."
—Simon Lovell, *How to Cheat at Everything*

The large number and types of scams and the number of people who have fallen prey should produce volumes about why people succumb to these activities. But surprisingly, there are quite few and most tend to be inconclusive. FINRA Investor Education Foundation conducted an investigation into why and how investors are scammed.[1]

Their findings in 2013 are both revealing and not just a little surprising.

Fraud researchers typically found that a very small percentage of survey respondents self-report that they have been victims of financial fraud. Let's face it: It's embarrassing. Most people truly believe that they are not susceptible to being conned, but as Simon Lovell told us, they're wrong!

The phenomenon of not reporting fraud is hard to reconcile with the volume of fraud seen by regulators and law enforcement agencies. In fact, according to one FINRA study, an estimated 37.8 million incidents of fraud took place in 2011, but authorities received just more than 1 million fraud complaints.[2] The key findings of the study include:

1. The ubiquity of fraud solicitations, coupled with the inability of many people to recognize the red flags of fraud, place a large number of Americans at risk of losing money to scams.

2. More than eight in ten respondents were solicited to participate in a potentially fraudulent offer, and 11 percent of respondents lost a significant amount of money after participating in such scams.

3. Americans sixty-five and older are more likely to be targeted by fraudsters and more likely to lose money once targeted. Older respondents were 34 percent more likely to have lost money than respondents in their forties.

4. Although 11 percent of respondents lost money in likely fraudulent activity, only 4 percent admitted to being a victim when asked directly,

an estimated under reporting rate of more than
60 percent.

A study conducted by psychologists Doug Shadel and
Karla Pak found consistencies to our FINRA research. The
work describes a series of fraud victims profiling studies,
comparing known victims to nonvictims. In doing so, it
seeks to identify factors that predict victimization in two
different types of fraud, while circumventing the problem
of victim denial.

According to the Shadel and Pak report:

1. Investment fraud victims are more likely to be
    financially literate, married, male, have a col-
    lege degree or more, earn $35,000 per year or
    more (2007 study), and are more open to "per-
    suasive appeals."
2. Lottery fraud victims are more likely to be
    female, widowed, and living alone; earn less
    than $30,000 per year; be less financially liter-
    ate; and "live for today."
3. When asked simply, only 10 to 20 percent of
    investment victims and a slightly larger per-
    centage of lottery victims would acknowledge
    having been defrauded (with the rate depend-
    ing on the question phrasing).
4. A secondary study of just investment victims
    was able to attain 62 percent acknowledgment
    using a "series of progressive, investment spe-
    cific questions."[3]

One of our operative variables in the opening chapter
is *subtlety*. So many people don't realize they've been had

and so many others are simply too embarrassed to admit that they've been victimized. We all have a measure of arrogance (or pride) that suggests "no, not me!"

My wife and I recently helped my eighty-nine-year-old uncle by placing him in an assisted living facility. I served as power of attorney for legal and financial matters. When my uncle's mail was redirected to me, I was astonished by the number of warranty programs, buyer's offers, credit card offers, and so forth mailed to him daily from legitimate-sounding nonprofit organizations. Oh, and so many of them having the implied or specific endorsement of AARP was troubling. Want to buy term insurance for an older American? If AARP is on the label it must be legit, right? For years before she died, my elderly mother would greet every cold call or solicitation with "My son takes care of all that. Call him." I never received a single call.

With 10,000 Americans turning sixty-five years of age every day this trend is troubling.[4] The bad guys are also abundantly aware of this trend as their "market" expands exponentially. Let's further explore the impact of aging and the reduced cognitive abilities to discern good offers from scams. And more importantly, how seniors can resist or get help from others.

In 2009, a study conducted by Carolyn Yoon, University of Michigan, Catherine Cole, University of Iowa and Michelle Lee, Singapore Management University, entitled "Decision Making and Aging," uncovered and established some "whys" behind senior decision-making.[5] In their work, the professors found that the older one gets, the more susceptible they are to poor decisions. Older consumers are more likely than young consumers to:

1. Respond to emotional material, personal infor-
    mation, familiar names, and big brands.
2. Forget the source of information (and thus mis-
    remember a fact as true).
3. Use rules of thumb, intuition, or "common.
    sense" to make decisions.
4. Make poor decisions under time pressure, later
    in the day, or when accompanied by references
    to negative stereotypes.
5. Delegate decision-making to others. (Witness
    my mother's strategy!)

From these three independent studies and countless
others we can deduce that the problem is certainly larger,
much larger, than most will even admit. It is subtle and
steeped in deception. The perpetrator has one goal and one
only: to deceive others and financially advantage themselves. So let's break it down.

Can we all agree that human beings are emotional and
that most decisions are made with at least a modest element of how we feel? Consumer advocates warn us never
go grocery shopping while we are either hungry or dis-
comforted. The reasons are obvious. We will make purchases that will satisfy our short-term hunger or purchases
that will bring us comfort. Both might be considered ill
advised. The number of times I walk into a grocery store
intending to buy one or two items, yet before I reach the
checkout counter my basket is full, is embarrassing. Henry
Ford had it all wrong when he said, "A customer can have
a car painted any color he wants as long as it's black." The
wide variety of automobile styles and colors speak to our

emotions and not practicality. If we could only make deci-sions devoid of emotions we might all be driving smaller automobiles designed exclusively to get us from one place to another. Why does a soccer mom (or dad) need a Range Rover to get the kids to practice—unless, of course, prac-tice is on the Serengeti? Could it be a need to impress? Call it panache, the way the car makes us feel. Or call it what it is: emotion.

Therein lies the dilemma. Greed and fear rule our buy-ing and selling habits with an iron hand. Why else would perfectly logical people be willing to buy into a raging bull stock market only to sell the same securities and compa-nies when the market falls? It's the same company at $20 per share as it was when we bought it at $30, only now it's truly on sale. Logic dictates that we should be buying more shares the same way we shop coupons and deals for items we need at the grocery or clothing store. And yet fear intro-duces such fierce emotion that we can't deny giving in, and we sell. Greed is likewise as powerful.

There's a certain element of seduction to a "story stock." A broker calls a prospect with the name of a new company that is destined to "revolutionize an industry." Perhaps it's a cancer-defeating drug that this startup company has just been granted FDA approval to begin testing. The broker will tell the person, "The last time something like this took place, people made millions. People were turn-ing $5,000 investments into $5 million in just a matter of weeks." Now, you either dismiss this as being improbable (although entirely possible) or you listen to more details. Who wouldn't want to be in on the ground floor of the next big thing? Quite possibly, one indeed might make several times their investment. And if you were fortunate enough to have been an early investor in Amazon, Apple, Microsoft, Google, or so many other names, you wouldn't be reading this book. You would be on your yacht. But our con man from the opening quotation of the chapter, Simon Lovell, writes, "Remember that greed is the hustler's greatest weapon. It may look like easy money but nothing in life is free."[6]

My point is that yes, opportunities abound in the marketplace, but to make a decision based on emotion—in this case, greed—is wrong and ill advised. Rather, coming to a decision carefully, side-stepping subtlety and armed with knowledge, we can make the same good choices while avoiding the bad ones. My oversimplified conclusion is that it is imperative to take as much emotion out of a decision as is humanly possible and replace it with knowledge. Only then can we avoid the subtle persuasions of people who want to advantage themselves at our expense.

Scams exact a huge toll on consumers and society at large, with annual costs in the United States alone exceeding $100 billion.[7] The global proliferation of the Internet has enabled con artists to export their craft to a rapidly expanding market and reach previously untapped consumers. In spite of the prevalence of scams around the world, there has been virtually no academic attention devoted to understanding the factors that might account for why individuals differ in scamming vulnerability. Proposed theory incorporates the effects of visceral influences on consumer response to scam offers and hypothesizes a role for various moderating factors such as self-control, gullibility, susceptibility to interpersonal influence, and scam knowledge. As the reader may interpret, this is all very nebulous and lacks empiricism because there are just way too many factors involved. The very best way we can minimize the opportunities for deception, especially as it pertains to older people, is to compile a plan of action that incorporates knowledge and a vigilant attitude.

Here are a few actions you could consider taking on your behalf or perhaps on behalf of a loved one.

1. Note that scammers have the greatest degree of success with older Americans who live alone or are otherwise isolated from family and friends. As the percentage of people considered senior (65 and older) grows, so does the market for the bad guys. If you are an older American and would like a further safeguard, enlist a family member or trusted advisor or attorney who will assist in making decisions. Perhaps a financial advisor or attorney or good friend would qualify and agree. If you tell a would-be scammer that you would like him to call "my advisor, Bill" you will never hear from him again. Legitimate service providers will have no problem speaking to someone else if it helps lead to a sale. I remember an elderly woman who I helped build a portfolio of tax-free bonds. I would call her and describe to her a municipal bond I thought would meet her expectations. She would listen intently and tell me to "call Ralph," her nephew who was an attorney. I looked forward to calling him to describe the bond, and he would typically agree that the bond fit his aunt's profile. What a great advantage for my client. If you have an elderly parent or grandparent,

please discuss with them this type of courtesy. "Nana, there are a lot of people out there who prey upon others. Why not give any of these people my phone number and ask them to call me? I would be happy to help you make some of these confusing decisions." I would then tell Nana the specific calls she might receive such as what I have described earlier. (e.g., "Nana, maybe someone wants to paint your house, clean your roof, or call you with an investment idea. Or maybe it's a charity that you are not familiar with.") A ninety-year-old gentleman I had the pleasure of advising was the perfect victim. Larry, a devout Catholic, could not say no to any organization that had the pretense of sounding Catholic. He was draining his savings. When I addressed this with him, he told me that it had to be for a good cause and he was happy to contribute. As he was quickly running out of money, I enlisted the support of his attorney and a trusted family member, who took over control of his checkbook. Yes, I took away some of Larry's independence, but it was the right thing to do. Larry never did run out of money.

2. Get off the phone grid! Sign up for the National Do Not Call Registry (donotcall.gov or 888-382-1222); it may not prevent all calls coming in from crooks, but it will certainly cut down on the number of calls you might otherwise receive unsolicited. There is also a service available to certain providers like Comcast and Time Warner called Nomorobo. Sign up

for this, or call your telephone service provider and ask if they offer a similar service.

3. Make certain you know your contractor. Each state has a contractor-licensing bureau, and a simple call can verify the contractor's license. Also, make sure they have proper insurance and bonding. *Never* pay in full up front. It is customary for a contractor to ask for one-third down before commencing on a project, but seldom should you give more than that. Ask for local references and don't be afraid to check with the Better Business Bureau. Both Angie's List and Home Advisors offer great intelligence on contractors by letting others who have had bad (or excellent) service describe their experience. Check out both these websites.

4. In the case of my uncle, as I earlier described, I took power of attorney prerogative over all his finances and paid his bills and settled all his legal matters. This is indeed extreme, but because of his physical and mental condition, it was necessary. Another measure of protection for elders might include setting up oversight to his or her accounts by asking that duplicate monthly statements be mailed to your attention. Additionally, one could establish a limited account on behalf of a loved one whereby they would have their own account but the total accessible would be limited to a certain dollar amount, say $500. All other expenditures could be paid from an account that you were cosignatory. (Make certain you

use the primary owner's Social Security number for tax purposes.)

5. Lastly, simply check in with your parents,
grandparents, friends, or loved ones. And
sometimes even arrive unannounced. Of course
you'll want to see if they are taking required
medications and their general physical health,
but the pop-in visit may reveal issues that are
unknown to you. Who's visited recently, do
they have any new "friends," and so forth? It's a
loving courtesy.

Can we deduce that the variables that influence our
poor decisions include naïveté, subtlety, fear, greed, age
(and accompanying decrease of mental acuity), and other
factors too modest to consider? Yes, and the intelligent person can greatly minimize the possibilities of fraud by being
ever mindful of these variables and ever vigilant. There are
a number of other studies designed to highlight scamming
techniques, and the whys and wherewithal behind them, but
suffice to say you and I have uncovered the principal ones,
the ones that the Madoffs among us know only too well.

Naïveté, fear, greed, and age are all about the potential victim. And of these four, three can be controlled. We
can't alter the aging process. Let's face it: The older we get,
the more we forget. And unfortunately, many hundreds of
thousands of people suffer from varying degrees of demen-
tia due to genetics, environment, or accidents.

So if we are truly prepared to make a commitment to
minimizing the probability of losing money, it's incumbent
upon us to address the three controllables: naïveté, fear,

and greed. Fortunately, all three can be addressed with the one thing that gives each of us power: knowledge.

Naïveté

When we relinquish our authority to an advisor because he or she simply knows more than we do, it may be because of an unwillingness to get informed. When an advisor tells us that we should "diversify into other asset classes," we accept this as being reasonable. It's certainly true that if one owns more than one class of security, one has a safer position. And it's reassuring to operate from a vantage point of safety but does this strategy match our personal objectives? Does the same asset allocation portfolio work for a thirty-year-old as a seventy-year-old? (No!)

Fear

On October 19, 1987, when the Dow Jones plunged more than 30 percent, everybody's first thought was to sell. After all, "we can't afford to lose any more money." I was at my desk on that day, and all but one incoming call gave me orders to sell, sell, sell! The one man who bought, did so at about 3:30 in the afternoon. He calmly came in, sat down, and bought as many high-quality companies as he could afford. I remember telling him that he was the bravest man of the day. He was hugely rewarded with his purchases because over the course of the next year, and certainly the next thirty years, his brave and contrarian buys paid him handsomely.

Greed

Ever wonder why lottery sales swell the week before a massive payoff? Greed! People want in. They're unwilling to risk a dollar for a mere million dollars even though the odds are infinitely better at winning (though still not very good). No, they want to wager ten dollars for the very unlikely chance of winning $500 million. And who doesn't want to own the next Amazon, Apple, or Microsoft? I'm reminded of the movie *The Wolf of Wall Street,* when Jordan Belfort (played by Leonardo Di Caprio) paints a glowing picture of a small "up and coming" company to some poor sucker on the phone. He made it sound pretty darn good and the victim bought. Greed begs the question, "What if this works? I'll be rich!"

=====

Does it take effort on our part? I'm afraid so, but by equipping ourselves with the right question, the right information, and the right measure of apprehension or skepticism, we can absolutely reduce the chance of fraud to an exponential extent.

CHAPTER 5

THE TOP SIX SCAMS IN AMERICA TODAY

"The lack of money is the root of all evil."
—Mark Twain

I t is important to remind ourselves that the Madoffs don many hats. Though the investment world typically is responsible for the most egregious and costly scams, there are other avenues of deceit designed to defraud and rob Americans of their hard-earned dollars. I have and will spend most of this composition dealing with financial advisory, but I would be remiss if I didn't remind you of other misdealings that impact a person's wealth.

The American Association of Retired Persons (AARP) not only identified six people found guilty of fraud but also identified six themes.[1] They are (in no particular order) romance, charity, grandparents, home repair, health care, and investment. Let's address these scams from the buyer's perspective.

Romance

Romance cost American women fifty years and older at least $34 million in 2012. Men fifty and older reported losing $5 million. These are the reported numbers.[2] Consider the number of people who never report these events because they are so embarrassing. A mother-daughter "team" from just outside Denver posted on dating websites as U.S. military personnel serving in Afghanistan.[3] Their ploy was to ask for money to pay for tickets home for a chance to meet. Over a three-year period, Karen and Tracy Vasseur made off with more than $1 million extracted from 374 people in the United States and forty other countries. In August 2013, mother Karen was sentenced to twelve years in state prison and daughter Tracy received a fifteen-year sentence. What could be more emotional than romance? The chance to meet and engage an attractive person on a personal basis is extremely compelling. It is also a pretty easy scam for a con person to activate. Colorado Attorney General John Suthers, upon sentencing told the press, "Not only did this mother-daughter duo break the law, they broke hearts worldwide. It is fitting that they received stiff sentences for their unconscionable crimes committed in the name of love and the United States military."

Charities

"This is John with Ohio Veterans Source. You have been generous in the past giving to veterans, and I was wondering if you could help out again. It means so much at Thanksgiving and Christmas."[4] John W. Hargrove targeted older people for a made-up charity he called "Ohio Veterans Source." Who doesn't want to help our vets? So a slick phone call or email solicitation or mailed request is often greeted with a certain respect. Suffice to say, it is never a good idea to donate money to a nonprofit you don't know anything about, nor give your credit card number to anybody you don't know. Hargrove was sentenced to two-and-a-half years and ordered to pay $2,000 in restitution. This same guy was convicted of the same crime six years previously. One has to be especially diligent when it comes to charities. There are so many excellent nonprofits that do such good work for people in need. And Americans are quite typically generous, so when someone calls or writes with a good sounding cause, we listen and often give. Perhaps the best advice comes from a sixty-five-year-old victim of Hargrove's scam who said she wrote two checks to his fake group. From now on, she said, she will give to only two charities she has a personal connection with. When others ask for donations, "I just say no."

An important question to have verified by an organization is how much of each dollar is allocated to the benefit of the needy. Is it eighty-five cents of each dollar or is it fifty cents? A large number of peripheral and sometimes illegal charities enrich themselves by taking exceptionally large percentages of each dollar donated. A better response is simply to say, "No, thank you," and contribute to a local charity you know very well. There are also websites (www.charity navigator.org and www.guidestar.org are two examples) that will help verify a nonprofit's effectiveness. Reading these groups opinions regarding specific charities might surprise most readers.

Grandparents

The by now famous "grandparents" scam that was perpetrated upon my friend is a classic. The bad guys collect personal information about family members from obituaries, social media, and ancestry websites. They often call late at night and pretend to be a grandchild who has been arrested or hospitalized and in dire need of immediate money. Michael Angelo Giuffrida of Canada was sentenced to a two-year prison term for his role as a "runner."[5] U.S. Border Patrol officers searching his car found $100,000 in travelers' checks and cash that had been recently redeemed from wire transfers. Most of the victims were in their eighties who feared for their grandkids' safety. One gentle grandmother lost more than $68,000. Being mindful and paying special attention to our parents and grandparents can go a long way to prevent this type of activity.

There are variations on this nefarious scam that might include a son or daughter being involved in a car accident with "dangerous" individuals like a gang member and unless reparations are paid immediately severe consequences could take place. As law enforcement officers will remind people, scammers play on your emotions. We typically react emotionally, rather than intellectually. I encourage the reader to take time and take a breath; don't become a victim.

It's always a good idea to slow down and call local police. Indeed our first reaction is emotional, and this is a tough variable to overcome. Call the police, call your children or parents, and call upon your intellect, denying your initial reaction. And again, the perpetrators prey upon older people, who may have diminished mental capacity. They've learned that older people, grandparents, just aren't as suspicious as younger people.

Home Repair

Someone driving by your home stops and knocks on your front door. "I'm a contractor and couldn't help but notice your roof (or siding, or trim or driveway, etc.) needs some work. I'm here doing work in the neighborhood and could do it pretty inexpensively." Often they demand 50 percent up front. If they return, you can expect them to find other parts of your home that may need repair. They are often unlicensed and prey on older homeowners. Randall Lee Joyner was part of a ring of ten people and is presently waiting trial in North Carolina.[6] When Joyner and others were apprehended they had bilked $300,000 from trusting souls. North Carolina Attorney General Roy Cooper said, "Con artists who prey on seniors have to be stopped." The average age of the victims that took place principally in North Carolina was eighty-five years old, and many of the cases involved scam artists pretending to be contractors who generally approach their targets to perform a general task, such as cleaning gutters, and then later tell them about a more serious problem "discovered" during their work.

Homeowners can use Angie's List, Home Advisors, the Better Business Bureaus, and even Yelp to determine if the firm is reputable. My wife and I live in coastal Virginia, and when a hurricane or storm hits, we are inundated with out-of-state "contractors" willing to assist with tree removal, home repair, and so forth. Some of these firms are very legitimate, albeit expensive, but there will always be the crop that intends to defraud.

Unfortunately, the criminals understand that emotion plays a major role in their success, so when a natural disaster occurs they come out in full force. People affected by hurricanes, floods, tornadoes, and the like are emotionally distraught and ripe for rip-off. The same rules apply: namely, resist the temptation to act emotionally, and do your homework. In 2002 Hurricane Isabel crushed the Virginia coastline. Our home was affected, with dozens of downed trees, some resting on our house. Three trees actually fell through one section of our home. When my wife and I returned to find the destruction, we simply wanted everything back to normal and immediately began to seek out help, as did everyone in a similar situation. The number of local contractors who could help was overwhelmed, and so hundreds of contractors from across the country poured into Hampton Roads to "help." Most were legitimate, but some were not. I definitely understand the feeling of helplessness (fear) that people feel in similar conditions.

Health care

Bruce H. Cherry, fifty-two, of Philadelphia pleaded guilty to charges of fraud and theft stemming from his role in a ring that scammed at least 218 people of $800,000, most of whom were in their eighties.[7] They sold fraudulent (bogus) contracts for nonmedical home care as a substitute for long-term health-care insurance. The four men indicted and convicted were Cherry, Ross M. Rabelow, Thomas J. Muldoon, and Robert P. Lerner. They sold service contracts that purportedly provided specialty services for seniors. Payment for services was due in advance, and the services were never provided because they simply didn't exist.

Pennsylvania Attorney General Linda Kelly said, "This was a disturbing and despicable scheme designed to extract as much money as possible from unwitting seniors who believed they were protecting themselves against costly future home-care expenses."

Medicare scams are very popular because they are not very well understood. AARP further cautions people to remain vigilant because of the many misconceptions regarding the Affordable Care Act. They anticipate an epidemic in the years to come. It's not surprising that the "marks," or victims, continue to be people of advanced age.

Investment

Need we say anymore? Let me tell you about a friend of mine who was in her late eighties. Her financial advisor, representing a well-respected national bank, told her that she should liquidate her considerable holdings in long-held stocks in favor of a variable annuity. The reasoning was simple: trade volatile positions for a guaranteed income benefit with tax advantages. Sound good? Sure, if you're a much younger investor who doesn't have a huge capital gain tax upon liquidating your stocks. But an eighty-eight-year-old widow? The advisor was trying to score a big commission with the sale of an insurance product that traditionally pays very handsomely. The woman's son-in-law, a client of mine, called me and questioned what had occurred. I advised my client to call the firm's branch manager immediately, describe the situation, and wait for his response. Fortunately, the manager made the client whole by backing off the trades. The bank's manager knew exactly what happened: A young advisor, new to the industry, thought he was going to generate a commission at the expense of an older client. Perhaps it was due to the advisor's lack of experience, but nonetheless it was the absolute wrong thing to do. Incidentally the woman passed away shortly thereafter, and her highly appreciated stocks passed tax-free to her heirs. Had she not had assistance from her son-in-law and me (and the branch manager), she would have incurred a huge capital gain tax, and the assets in the annuity would be subject to tax to her beneficiaries. This is a subtler example of investment misrepresentation.

There is one ploy that I urge everyone to be keenly aware of. This is when the investment advisor asks the investor to liquidate their account because he or she has better investment returns or opportunities "outside of the company."

You recall the lesson of Monica, my financial advisor trainee, from the introduction? That's where she asked clients to invest in her new venture. These investments would be used to build her securities business. In essence, the investments were unregistered and considered "selling away," a term used in the industry to describe any investment that is outside the financial firm's purview. This happens more often than one would think.

Witness Jane E. O'Brien, sixty-two, of Needham, Massachusetts. O'Brien was convicted in 2013 for absconding with $250,000 from a client.[8] In April 2015, O'Brien pleaded guilty to multiple counts of mail fraud, wire fraud, and investment advisory fraud in connection with a scheme to defraud several clients. She simply accepted funds with the promise to invest and kept the money for her own personal use. O'Brien caused one client to first empty her brokerage account and give the proceeds to O'Brien, and then to borrow an additional $1 million on her home and give much of that money to her to invest. O'Brien had been employed by Merrill Lynch and Smith Barney but convinced clients to give her their money to invest in businesses outside Merrill Lynch. Once she was in possession of the funds, she used them for her personal purposes and benefit. She is serving six years in prison.

And here's one last unnerving example.

Jim Staley, a pastor from St. Charles, Missouri, who served as a financial advisor, made away with $3.3 million.[9] His church, Passion for Truth Ministries, may have been perfectly legitimate, but that didn't keep Staley from stealing from elderly clients. He contended that he did not hurt anyone from his own congregation, but some victims and their relatives in court called him "sick, manipulative and deceitful." They said that some elderly investors trusted him because of his professed Christian faith and family values. "I was not conning little old ladies out of their money," he said. "I was in the wrong place at the wrong time." His sins were promising guaranteed returns and persuading some to cash in annuities knowing it would result in substantial sums lost to penalties. He also falsely claimed that Warren Buffett was an investor and that companies were using the investments in their 401(k) plans. He is now serving seven years on four counts of wire fraud.

It begs the question . . . Whom do you trust?

The constant among all six scams can be summed up in one word: emotion. Romance preys upon people's need for love and acceptance. Being charitable makes us feel good about ourselves as we help others. Grandparents share such a bond with their grandchildren and are protective because of the love they have for them. Even home repair takes advantage of a person's emotions. ("What if the roof falls in?" or "This sounds like such a good opportunity.") And all of us are in touch with our mortality and health, and most place this as a top priority, oftentimes denying the reality of financial resources or lack thereof. And finally, investments that are governed by fear and greed. Warren Buffett famously proclaimed, "Be fearful when others are greedy. Be greedy when others are fearful."[10] If only it were that simple, but witness what has occurred in the markets.

In 1999 the technology sector had defied all odds and was trading at record highs. Investors continued to buy believing that there was a "new economy," only to be crushed by reality during the ensuing months and years. All markets eventually seek equilibrium, and the early years of the twenty-first century proved no exception. But you couldn't tell investors to stay away because the promise of riches—and often "quick riches" is too emotionally compelling.

I recall a young man in his thirties who had made a great deal of "paper profit" in his stock portfolio. (Paper profit is reading one's brokerage statement from month to month as it accelerates in appreciation. It's never a true profit until the investor sells and "realizes" the gain.) This man was so convinced that his portfolio and the market in general would continue to advance that he encouraged his family members to "buy technology." His sixty-five-year-old uncle was bitten by the greed bug and took out a second mortgage on his home—a home that was mortgage free—and bought into his nephew's hysteria. You know what happened next. The market crashed, and all his uncle had left was a new and large debt that would greatly impede his ability to live comfortably. Greed is a powerful adversary to logic and good decision-making, challenged only by its cousin, fear. In other words, your emotions.

As of this writing the Dow Jones is trading at historic highs. Is this a result of increased corporate earnings, euphoria, or both? Knowing how much emotion is built into the market, your author remains suspicious and advises caution.

The corpus of this book is to help Americans avoid losing money by controlling these two adversaries: by recognizing subtlety and by applying knowledge and discipline. That's why I have devoted such a large percentage of this work to the investment business. After all, the largest number of potential opportunities for scams are inherent in the financial services industry simply because such a large percentage of Americans are invested in the financial marketplace. It is also the industry wherein I have spent my entire professional career, thus enabling me to provide you with tangible and real examples. The aforementioned five additional themes of fraud identified by AARP are also important to consider, but because of my personal experience and the number of people who have invested assets in the financial services industry, I believe this will best serve the majority of readers.

When and if you have a call or visit from one of the six notorious scams or even some of the twenty-first-century's "new and improved" scams (such as back taxes owed to the IRS, real estate taxes due, breached security to your computer, even reverse mortgage ploys, etc.) take the following actions:

1. **Be suspicious.** If the caller wants money right away, I don't care how intense the situation, don't do it. Take a deep breath and time to digest. The caller's intent is to get you as upset as he or she can. Personal information is typically what the scammer wants. This is a red flag and is reason to be especially suspicious. Information such as Social Security number, credit cards numbers, login or passwords for your computer belongs to you but gives access to the bad guys to your most personal information.

2. **Call your closest relatives and confidants.** Many people who have received such calls will actually call the child or grandchild in question and make certain they are okay. Here's where you need a team. Lean on them.

3. **Stay informed.** Read the many resources regarding how people lose money so that if you receive such a call, you will be reminded that this is probably dirty.

May I tell you something from personal experience and corroborated by factual documentation? Investors are terrible at their own decisions. And worse, investor education is considered "futile," at least by the well-respected, Boston-based Dalbar Company. In their recently released annual *Quantitative Analysis of Investor Behavior,* Dalbar offers the following conclusion:

Attempts to correct irrational investor behavior through education have proved to be futile. The belief that investors will make prudent decisions after education and disclosure has been totally discredited. Instead of teaching, financial professionals should look to implement practices that influence the investor's focus and expectations in ways that lead to more prudent investment decisions.[11]

Dalbar has the distinction of thirty years of measuring the attitudes and actions of investors. They are highly sought after when financial services companies need new data regarding potential clients. And over those thirty years from 1983 through 2013, what Dalbar uncovered is disturbing. The Standard & Poor 500 returned 11.11 percent annually, but the lowly individual investor achieved only 3.69 percent annually. The bottom line and essential problem is that investors tend to sell their investments when markets go down (fear) and buy the same investments back when markets go up (greed).

Dalbar's president and CEO, Lou Harvey adds, "It is astounding that after all the evidence of failure to teach individuals to make prudent decisions, the belief remains that more spending on education and disclosures will eventually work."[12]

Perhaps the best weapon, maybe the only weapon, is not expertise in all matters financial but in a thorough understanding of our personal limitations coupled with the counsel of a trusted financial fiduciary.

Understanding that we are *all* potential victims. Understanding that if an opportunity is too good to be true, it probably is. Understanding that on subjects where we lack experience or solid resource, we better let it go.

Understanding that our emotions govern most of our decisions and this is virtually impossible to separate us from who we are.

We've all heard that the best defense is a good offense. And I propose that the very best way to develop an effective offense is with understanding. I posit that one need not have a financial background to make excellent financial decisions. One also need not rely completely on the advice of his or her financial advisor, but rather, a collaborative effort focusing on the investor's own temperament, ability to weather market volatility, and the comfort that comes with understanding.

I'm not certain just what it is but some people (maybe it's left-brained people?) can appreciate financial concepts and ratios more quickly than their cerebral antagonists (right-brained people). My very intelligent wife, who will be quick to remind me that her IQ, college GPA, and high school SATs were all higher than mine, glosses over when I ask her to review our financial and estate matters. She finds this information boring, hard to understand, and not especially interesting. She trusts me to do the research before we discuss our finances and essentially make the final decisions. (More on that later. I'm flattered, but I may not be around as long as she.) I, on the other hand, love to read financials and industry-specific journals and periodicals. Is that because I'm not as smart?

So, how about an intelligent, objective conversation with our financial advisor? A conversation whereby we can readily understand the basics and the intent and even probable outcome. The financial services industry needs to insist on a conversation designed to focus all attention on the needs and expectations of you, the client. Dalbar's findings conclude that education is at best, hit and miss. So let's just talk about our financial needs to an honest, caring advisor.

This is indeed possible, and I submit that this conversation takes place thousands of times per day throughout the country. Well-intended, well-informed advisors presenting financial options designed to meet clients' objectives, understanding, and comfort is the standard. You deserve at least the standard. It's up to you to make certain you're working with the right advisor.

The six top scams in America are by no means the only ones we need to be aware of.

Sagar Thakkar (aka "Shaggy") of Thane, India, is the alleged mastermind behind a $300-million-dollar IRS scam.[13] His scam, based in India and employing more than 700 people between 2013 and 2017, targeted thousands of Americans. The caller or "robo caller" left an alarming message for the victim. "This is the Internal Revenue Service calling. Your past due tax must be cleared up immediately to avoid arrest. Call the following number to speak with an IRS agent." Thakkar and his cohorts knew that the mere suggestion of owing the IRS money conjures fear among American taxpayers, and that's exactly the emotion they were going for. Once the victim returned the call, it was game on for the call center con person. They would pick a number and demand payment be made to avoid the local police from knocking on their door. Payment could be made with wire transfer, using their credit or debit card or even gift cards. This is yet another terrible example of the subtle reaching the naïve and introducing the emotion of fear. An informed victim would realize that the Internal Revenue Service just doesn't operate this way and would never simply call and demand payment. They would certainly not ask for payment over the phone, but they would send a registered letter to the taxpayer and request further corroborating information or maybe an audit to substantiate their claim for additional taxes. And yet, more than 15,000 U.S.-based taxpayers were conned, and more than 450,000 were on the list of potential marks.

I received three such calls this past year. My caller ID indicated a Washington, DC, address. It may not have been from Thakkar's group, as there are literally dozens set up around the world. I took it a step further: I called back and spoke with a man. I played along for a few minutes and must have offended him, because he told me to take my money and "put it where the sun doesn't shine."

I really don't recommend playing with these thieves, so I suggest simply hanging up and perhaps calling the local police. The Federal Bureau of Investigation has a website where you can also report such a disturbing event. But here's the rub: Authorities in the United States have little recourse to prevent this from happening and certainly from overseas. Therefore it's incumbent upon the consumer, the taxpayer, the potential victim to remind themselves, "I can be conned, so don't let emotion get in the way, and let me learn more about this." The Internet is a great source of information about numerous scams, and a simple Google search would lead a suspicious person to IRS scams and how to react. The bad guys don't want you to get that far, so they insist on urgency of response.

The United States government publishes a very helpful website (IRS.gov) warning of the most recent scams and how to deal with each. In the wake of Hurricane Harvey that devastated Houston and the Gulf Coast, the site's first warning read. "Hurricane Harvey scams: Callers lie about flood insurance," and robo calls tell homeowners and renters that their flood premiums are past due. The scammers have no conscience and fewer scruples. They are interested in money—your money—and will stoop as low as they can to steal from you.

On this important site, you browse scams by topics such as cars, charity, credit and loan offers, debt relief, investment, lottery and sweepstakes, online dating, phishing, and weight loss, to name just a few.

CHAPTER 6

FIVE MOST IMPORTANT QUESTIONS TO ASK YOUR FINANCIAL ADVISOR

*"Learn from yesterday, live for today,
hope for tomorrow. The important
thing is not to stop questioning."*
—Albert Einstein

Effective advisors will ask their clients many questions. They endeavor to find out as much as possible about you and your family. New York Stock Exchange Rule 405 reads, "a registered representative must know their client for the purpose of making suitable recommendations."[1] Likewise, FINRA has Rule 2090, which admonishes advisors to "know their client." Specifically, this rule requires "firms use reasonable diligence in regard to the opening and maintenance of every account, to know the essential facts concerning every customer." The rule further explains, "essential facts" are "those required to effectively service the customer's account and in accordance with any special handling instructions for the account, understand the authority of each person acting on behalf of the customer, and comply with applicable laws, regulations and rules."[2] The "know your customer" obligation arises at the beginning of the customer-broker relationship and does not depend on whether the broker has made a recommendation.

I believe your advisor better ask a lot of questions. These questions are beyond your age, marital status, occupation, salary, tax bracket, and so forth. Questions should include your investment experience, comfort level with potentially volatile investments, savings, children, grandchildren, estate planning, and charitable inclinations, to mention just a few. It is incumbent upon an advisor to truly know their client, and the only way to do that is to ask a lot of questions.

But this should never be one-sided. How about "know your advisor"? Why is it that so few of us bother to ask our advisor questions that will provide insight into who they are, their lives, their investment process, their teams, how often will they contact us, and their fees? This is only fair, and if an advisor resists answering any of these important questions, it's time to move on. My experience and opinion are that most will be happy to answer whatever questions one might have. Following are the five questions that you must ask.

1. "Tell me about your experience in the financial services business."

This question is designed to be open-ended and serve as a basis for discussion. An advisor may tell you he or she has been in the business for twenty years. Press the question: "Have you always been with your present firm?" This is an important question. There are very good reasons why an advisor might make a move to another company. Lack of support, the branch manager was a jerk, I couldn't service my clients as I felt appropriate; these are a few of the reasons you may hear. They may be perfectly legitimate. The fact that an advisor switches firms is not a crime.

Some advisors make a habit of moving from firm to firm every five years. I know these people and they are moving because the new firm is paying them a lot of money to "move their book" (that's you and all their other clients). Financial companies generate revenue based on "assets under management," and they buy assets much like any business that intends to grow. It's a great business model, but it may not necessarily benefit clients. It is an honest question to ask. You want to make certain your advisor is happy with his or her broker dealer or registered investment advisory company and intends to remain there for many years subject to conditions. If your advisor moves to another firm, a literal war breaks out between the acquiring firm and the company the advisor is leaving. Clients will receive numerous phone calls and written correspondence, all in an effort to persuade you to either stay with your advisor and move your account to the new company or remain with your present company and be introduced to a new advisor.

This is an important decision and should be approached very carefully. If you are fortunate enough to have a great relationship with your advisor, your decision is easier but still begs due diligence on your part. "Why are you moving?" I never left my very first firm, Legg Mason, because they provided me with everything my clients and I could ever need or want. As branch manager one of my responsibilities was to recruit advisors from the competition. I admonished each potential recruit by telling them that the only reason to switch firms is because your clients, your family, and you personally are advantaged. This might include a more accommodating office environment and more helpful manager or better access to money management. It's critical to note that the worst reason an advisor might give is to collect a check. Advisors are paid handsomely to bring their revenue stream (you) to another company. If an advisor is producing $800,000 in revenue, called trailing twelve months, a competitor company may be willing to hand the advisor a check for $1.2 million, or one-and-a-half trailing twelve. Is this wrong? No, it's how the business is structured, but it should never be the primary reason for moving. As inconvenient as it is for the advisor, it may also be inconvenient for the client because you'll be receiving at least two 1099 tax forms (one from each company), and you may not have access to some of the investments you enjoyed with the first firm. This is why I want you to ask your advisor or potential advisor, "Have you always been with XYZ broker dealer" and if not, "How many companies have you been with?" This information is a matter of public record, and you can find out by accessing brokercheck.com and simply typing in the advisor's name and city. Another honest question might be "How does this move benefit me and my family, and how does it affect my financial goals?"

2. "Do you have specific industry credentials such as CFP,® ChFC, or any others?"

In addition to the certifications I outline in Chapter 7, many firms have ordained their own certification programs. The advisor may tell you that he or she is a wealth management advisor or wealth consultant. Ask what this course of study entailed and what area(s) of wealth management expertise he or she possesses. Candidly, when I served as director of wealth management for my firm, we sponsored such a program. It was excellent and challenging, and it prepared our advisors to be sensitive to a wide variety of issues facing investors and taxpayers. It did not, however, prepare advisors to be expert in all matters.

There are some advisors who are really very good at investment selection and management. They may be ardent students of the markets and possess excellent skills. If you want a broker who buys and sells positions for gain, this might work for you, but most people need a "financial advisor" and not a "stockbroker." My personal bias is toward professionals who take their responsibilities seriously enough to continue their education so they might have advantage of the most recent and accurate financial and legal information available. This only enhances the advisor-client experience and speaks volumes about the advisor's commitment.

When an advisor embarks on a course of study, such as Certified Financial Planner, it may take one year to several years to complete. Such is the degree and depth of information necessary for successful completion. The newly minted CFP advisor has had comprehensive exposure and education in all matters pertaining to comprehensive planning. Among these areas are insurance and risk management, tax minimization, investments, estate planning, retirement, cash management, and financial planning. As a Certified Financial Planner, I can honestly attest to the difficulty and time involved in attaining this distinction and the confidence it brings to the advisor when helping clients.

There are many other excellent designations that serve to educate advisors, but the important constant is that the advisor wants to better serve the needs of his or her clientele.

3. "Tell me about your approach to financial planning."

The desired response from the advisor should sound something like this: "My investment approach is to meet the financial needs of each individual client. I want my clients to feel comfortable and confident with our plan design."

All advisors are not equal. Some have superlative education and credentials but lack the willingness (or ability) to make their clients feel the comfort that is so necessary. Other advisors are terrific at being personal but really don't have a clue about how best to help you achieve your goals. And a (very) few are simply out to enrich themselves at your expense. This is why a deliberate discussion about the advisor's approach to financial planning is imperative to understand. And I'd take it a step further. Ask, "Will I receive a written investment policy statement?" I really appreciate a financial professional who takes the time to put, in writing, exactly what a person can expect.

An investment policy statement might include the following:

- The advisor's philosophy regarding investing.
- Your investment objectives.
- Time horizons for cash flow or withdrawals.
- Risk levels.
- Investments including percentages (asset allocations) and whether they will be mutual funds or individual stocks and bonds.
- Consequences of taxation.
- How often we will meet.
- Duties and responsibilities of the advisor (and you as client).
- Any further disclosures.

An investment policy statement, as I'm sure you'll agree, puts everything on the table and in plain language. It leaves little doubt as to just how your money and financial welfare will be considered.

If there are ten advisors in an office, there may very well be ten different opinions on market conditions. The markets matter and, as we all know, and the markets will fluctuate. Of course markets impact our abilities to meet our personal financial needs, but the principal reason to invest for most Americans is to meet your financial goals and expectations. When an advisor suggests that the Dow Jones is due for a correction and I am positioning assets accordingly, the question should be "How so?" If the advisor is selling all growth assets like stocks in favor of cash, the next question is "How does this strategy help my financial goals?" The advisor may be absolutely correct, and the market just might drop, but no one knows when the markets will rise or fall. J.P. Morgan was once asked as he stepped out for lunch in New York one day, "Mr. Morgan, what is the market doing today?" He responded, "It's fluctuating."

4. "Will I be working with you personally or another member of your team?"

The industry has matured considerably due to bull markets that have dominated the economy since 1982 (with exception, of course). As a result, many advisors have leveraged their efforts by teaming with others or by hiring a team to assist their efforts. Both have proven to be necessary and very smart. But if the lead advisor, perhaps the person you have just met, has 1,000 client relationships, it's improbable that he or she will be able to devote a whole lot of attention to you and your account—unless, of course, you qualify as one of his or her largest accounts. And if this is you, you should fully expect a full complement of services and professional considerations. As an advisor, my single-largest client had in excess of $150 million entrusted with me. I had weekly contact with this gentleman, and when he called he always received immediate attention. My team was also instructed to respond with utmost courtesy, efficiency, and professionalism to all our clients, but especially to him.

Don't get your feelings hurt if you are not going to be working specifically with the lead advisor, but make certain you are abundantly comfortable working with another competent member of their staff. There were many clients who would call my office and ask for one of my assistants.

The client knew that I might be otherwise engaged and also that one of my team members would be quite capable of, and maybe even better at, answering a question than I. Clients need to have a personal connection with someone who is caring and intimate with their financial needs. This is where the wisdom of an investment policy statement comes into view. It leaves little doubt as to what you can expect.

Most team members are licensed and registered, and thus have an excellent understanding of financial matters and markets. My question is: Do they have an excellent understanding of you and your needs? If so, you've got a great ally on the team. I recall many of my clients calling one of my teammates first because they liked her and trusted her ability to answer their concerns. That's one great teammate!

5. "How do you charge for your services?"

This is a critical question but should never be your lead question. Advisors' and their respective firms' charges may vary greatly. There is a great deal of discretion that can be exercised when it comes to how an advisor is to be compensated for services.

According to Personal Capital, an online advisory firm, an average $500,000 investment account held for 30 years would pay roughly $500,000 to $1 million in fees, depending on the institution. The range was between just over 1 percent to almost 2 percent charged by various firms. The study assumed a 7 percent rate of return resulting in the client's $500,000 initial investment growing to $3.8 million in thirty years, not adjusting for inflation.[3] If this same account had not been charged $500,000 to $1 million, the savings would be in the client's account. Now, it's impossible to invest anywhere without incurring expenses, but my premise is to help the reader minimize the cost paid to the advisor or broker and maximize the amount accrued to the investor.

Let's talk a little about fee only versus fee based. Fee only has more recently been popularized and is a direct and usually hourly fee that is levied for providing direction to a client's wealth management. For instance, a couple with $750,000 of investable assets, three children, and a net worth of $1.25 million have questions and need objectivity to secure a level of comfort with their current financial disposition. They engage a fee-only advisor who charges them $2,500 for a comprehensive evaluation replete with specific recommendations regarding an asset allocation model of investments. The advisor completes a series of interviews and analysis with the couple and determines that they need to complete an estate plan that includes a revocable living trust, an increase in the amount of life insurance on both husband and wife, and a redirect for their investable assets after determining that the couple will not meet their intended goals.

The advisor will probably not help beyond this point and may advise them to seek the counsel of an attorney, an insurance professional, and the services of a no-load mutual fund company. The advisor may provide some or all of the services for a further fee, either commissions or fee based. This approach is for a more confident person or family that simply needs some direction and not ongoing advice. Please remember that markets and individual needs change all the time and that a financial plan, once in place, needs to be monitored and adjusted on a regular basis. The couple may reengage the fee-only advisor annually or every few years to make certain all is well. There will be additional charges, usually on an hourly basis.

A fee-based relationship is, or should be, far more comprehensive, and it implies ongoing and sustained service. This means that your advisor is at your beck and call when changes are necessary. This advisor will charge an annual fee based on the assets under management. For instance, the same $750,000 under management might be subject to a 1 percent fee, meaning that each and every year your account is subject to a $7,500 charge. If your assets grow, so does the advisor's fee ($1 million at 1 percent is $10,000, etc.). And if your assets depreciate, so does your fee. This is very popular in the business, and most firms advocate this arrangement because it "evens out" the budgeted revenue to the company and to the advisor. It also puts the advisor and the client in an equitable position. The more he or she is able to grow your account, the greater his or her compensation.

When you deal with most firms, you are dealing with entities that expect revenues and profits. This is perfectly acceptable. I don't want my money with a company that loses money. But there is a trade-off: You, as client, are paying not only the advisor but also the office expenses, the corporate expenses, the shareholder dividends, the corporate taxes, and any additional expenses that are incurred. That's a lot of money, and even at a modest 1 percent you have to determine if you are receiving good value. And if you are receiving good advice and constant communication, and feel confident that the advisor knows you and your family and is willing to do whatever it takes to help you achieve your goals, you probably have a good person helping your efforts. If, however, your advisor does not know you and your feelings, your family, and your expectations, or rarely calls you, you need to find another advisor—someone who is more deserving of the fees you're paying.

Here's an important note. If you are currently in a fee-based account *and* you are paying commissions, fire the advisor. This is double-dipping, and it does occur. In a fee-based account you are entitled to institutional share classes of mutual fund management. Most mutual funds can be sold or owned as *A, B, C,* or *I* classes. (There are other shares that various fund companies represent that are unique to the share classes referenced.)

A shares have the largest up-front charge and, depending on the size of the investment, just might be the very fairest way to own a fund. If a person invests $1 million, there may be absolutely no charge to the buyer and nominal ongoing expenses.

B shares have no up-front charge but typically have a hefty carrying charge and limit your access to your (own) money for a period. Surrender charges may be imposed if redemption of your shares occurs before the surrender period is over. Surrender fees are costs that a fund owner must subtract from sale of shares if one decides to sell earlier than the fund's prospectus dictates. B shares were popular in the 1980s and early 1990s but have fallen out of favor with the consumer.

C shares have no up-front charge, charge an annual fee (maybe 1.5 percent), and usually have a one-year surrender fee. This class is quite popular, but if the 1.5 percent charge is in addition to the advisor's fee of 1 percent, it becomes very expensive and quickly eats into the return of the portfolio.

I shares (institutional shares) are typically the very least expensive, and if you are in a fee-based account, you must insist that your share class be in this category. An advisor who is charging 1 percent (+/–), is in regular communication with a family, and truly understands the needs of his or her clients is truly worth keeping.

Having described the previous, permit me to help further by saying that understanding the many nuances of how an advisor charges is completely subjective. How engaged is the advisor? How well does he or she understand your family's needs? How proficient is the advisor relative to overall wealth management? I'm willing to pay for advice if it not only saves me tax dollars but also helps me leverage my efforts to make future wealth.

A friend of mine charges a 2 percent annual fee, but he includes advice on real estate, corporate cash needs, personal estate management, risk management, and many other aspects of comprehensive wealth management. It's expensive, but his clients don't object because of the extreme level of service he provides. When engaged in the important discussion of expenses there are actually two questions:

1. "How do you charge?"

    Are the charges fee only, fee based, commission, or some combination thereof? Is it a one-time or hourly charge? Is it based on my total assets under management? What class mutual funds will I own in my account?

2. "How much do you charge?"

    Is it a one-time charge of $2,500 for a comprehensive plan? How much each time we meet thereafter to update? If I place $500,000 with you, what percentage will my account be charged annually? (And, if so, will there be additional mutual fund management expenses?)

You might add a third question: "All in, including fund management costs, asset under management expenses and commissions, how much will I pay you each year?"

The financial services business is a multi-billion-dollar industry that employs many hundreds of thousands of people. They deserve to be paid. But *you* deserve to know how and how much you are paying. You have choices, not only with whom you work, but also how much you are willing to pay. That's what competition is all about, and knowledge is power—the power to choose the most competitive honest relationship you can find. It may be of interest to note that the top three reasons investors give for changing advisors do not include costs or fees. It is certainly a variable but of far less import to the average investor.

According to the Spectrum Group, 58 percent of high-net-worth investors have switched financial advisors during their lifetime and 23 percent have done so within the past five years. The three predominant reasons people gave for changing are:

- 24 percent cited lack of proactive contact.
- 23 percent said the advisor had not provided them with good ideas and advice.
- 22 percent switched advisors because the old one was underperforming compared with the overall stock market.[4]

Why is it that fees do not play a more predominant part in people's decision to continue a professional relationship with a certain advisor? Perhaps they do not realize or understand just how much or how they are being charged. Over a thirty-year period, fees play an incredibly large role, so it should be an important consideration.

CHAPTER 7

THREE FINANCIAL ADVISORS TO AVOID

"Associate yourself with people of good quality,
for it is better to be alone than in bad company."
—Booker T. Washington

We've established that it is impossible to discern with 100 percent assuredness the good advisors from the bad. It is, however, quite possible to avoid a swath of advisors who are either too inexperienced or too typical of a problem personality. This is the starting point. Recall the young advisor who wanted to sell all the highly appreciated stock in an eighty-year-old woman's portfolio in favor of an annuity. I want to believe the advisor was simply lacking experience and not doing this intentionally because the trade would be inexcusable. But this is a real risk. Or the advisor who is so slick that that you wonder if he or she is in the right business. Perhaps it's the person who is so emotionally attached to a belief that he or she fails to objectively make decisions. These three types of advisors deserve a hard look.

The Novice

Regardless the profession, we all start out as novices. A surgeon has a first patient, an accountant has a first tax return, and a financial advisor has his or her first prospect or client. Most advisors have successfully completed the registered representative exam administered by the New York Stock Exchange. That person then qualifies to enter a training program sponsored by most firms. This is a serious proposition. Not only must the new advisor possess above-average intelligence, he or she must have the acumen to listen carefully and thoughtfully to clients. If this person is armed with a good grasp of the markets and the ability to objectively consider the best course of action, I dare say you've chosen the right financial partner. But this new advisor is a rarity. The learning curve is steep and requires much more than an engaging personality. The very best newer advisors, in my opinion, are the ones who have joined a team of more experienced advisors. This novice should have the advantage of a mentor and be able to ask important questions of the senior advisors regarding investments and financial planning. These newer advisors should provide an investor with an enhanced sense of confidence.

I recall returning from my three-week training class and receiving a "lead" from my branch manager. A lead is the name of an individual who has requested more information on a product or service. The person who mailed in the postcard wanted more information about a unit investment trust (UIT). I studied about UITs and learned more about them during my training, but I was really in no position to drill down with a potential client and explain not only the benefits but also the risks. I called the person who had requested the information and tried to field his questions as best I could. Needless to say, I was nervous, ill prepared, and not at all surprised when the would-be buyer said no to my offer to add it to his portfolio. Chalk that one up to inexperience and lack of knowledge.

Another time as I was building my business, I knocked on the door of a midsize manufacturing company for the purpose of introducing myself to see if I might be of service. (This was a customary marketing technique and was encouraged by my firm.) I remember meeting the CEO of the company in his mahogany-walled office and thinking to myself, "What do I say now? This person is obviously successful, probably wealthy, and knows more about finance than do I." So when he introduced himself, I lit into a tirade intended to impress even the smartest of people. "Good morning. My name is Bill Francavilla. I'm an investment advisor, and I wanted to tell you about our inventory of tax-exempt municipal bonds with a coupon of 5 percent. The taxable equivalent yield for someone in your tax bracket is closer to 8 percent and it has call protection for fifteen years. It has a AA rating, thus demonstrating its creditworthiness."

I felt pretty good about myself. I reported this in a confident and professional manner, and I was certain I had impressed this gentleman to the point he would be interested in owning some of these bonds. He looked at me and said, "Young man, I have no idea what you're talking about." I had just committed a typical rookie mistake: assuming the person with whom I was speaking understood the language of my industry.

I was guilty of selling, not solving. I had no idea what his needs were or what financial objectives he and his family might have. As a newer advisor I had to sell to generate income, of course. A newer advisor doesn't have the luxury of a more level stream of income, as does an advisor with more time in the business. I wasn't desperate, but I was motivated to build a book of business. As I mentioned earlier, there are reasons why this may not be a concern if the new advisor works in conjunction with a seasoned team of other advisors who have the ability to monitor his or her activities and advise them accordingly. I will say that a newer person will have the time to hopefully provide you with a great deal of service. After all, they only have a handful of clients.

Do you recall my story about the client who had "complete confidence" in my abilities even though it was my first month in the business? She should have asked me about my experience in the business, my approach, and how I charge. Novices often "sell" the mutual funds, stocks, income ideas, and alternatives that they have recently been exposed to. So you may have an appointment with this advisor after he or she has had lunch with a wholesaler touting the latest and greatest master limited partnership. Guess what he or she will pitch? The master limited partnership—because this is what they now understand best.

If the novice is new only to the firm or even the industry but possesses a solid understanding of the financial planning process and they satisfactorily answer the five questions discussed in Chapter 6, then you may want to take the next step of establishing a professional relationship. Remember: All advisors were novice at one time. You don't have to dismiss all newbies, just be extra careful. These are your funds!

The Strongly Opinionated

We want our advisors to be in the know when it comes to market conditions. It's one of the reasons we hire their expertise. We don't want them to be a "perma-bear," one who is adamant about the impending market crash and can qualify his or her opinions with charts, history, and so forth. This advisor may be absolutely right, but people who portend to see the future are usually very, very wrong.

Likewise, we don't want a perma-bull who, regardless of current conditions, will always tell you that a long-term buy and hold strategy will consistently earn more appreciation. This advisor may be 100 percent correct as well, but remember that the self-proclaimed prescient personality will at some point implode. The expression "Even a broken clock is right twice a day" comes to mind. Invariably all people have certain preclusions relative to social, religious, and market conditions. But the only one of these that has a degree of quantification is the market because we can calculate our values daily.

As I continue to read and study markets, I am constantly reminded of the disparity of adamant viewpoints expressed by very intelligent experts. I don't doubt his or her path to conclusion but someone's going to be very wrong. For example, let's consider the musings of two market analysts,

namely Jeremy Siegel, the Wharton School professor who
wrote *Stocks for the Long Run* (McGraw-Hill, 1984), and
Jim Rogers, who in 2013 wrote *Street Smarts: Adventures on
the Road and in the Markets* (Crown Business, 2013). Both
authors make very strong cases for their respective positions. Siegel goes back to 1801 and argues that a dollar
invested in equities grew to $599,605. Bonds and gold grew
to $952 and ninety-eight cents, respectively. Pretty conclu-
sive, wouldn't you say? Rogers, on the other hand, makes
the case for getting out and staying out of most equities
going forward. He tells readers not to look to Wall Street
but to rather look to Main Street America: "There's going to
be a huge shift in American society, American culture, in
the places where one is going to get rich. The stockbrokers
are going to be driving taxis. The smart ones will learn
to drive tractors so they work for the smart farmers. The
farmers are going to be driving Lamborghinis." He makes
a compelling case for owning commodities, raw materials,
and natural resources. And who can argue with a guy who
cofounded the Quantum Fund (along with George Soros)?
Between 1970 and 1980 the portfolio gained 4,200 percent
while the S&P 500 Index advanced about 47 percent.[1]

Incidentally, the period from 2000 through the fall of
2016 saw stocks grow 42.1 percent.[2] There are times, however, when gold and other asset classes such as bonds have
grown far more rapidly. Are you willing to speculate, or are
you satisfied with having your financial plan in comfortable positions?

I can make the case for either position. I can convinc-
ingly argue that an investor should or should not be posi-
tioned in either stocks or commodities. I'm entitled to my
opinion, but I never have the right to impose my opinions

on a client's portfolio and financial goals. It must work the other way around. Armed with what you tell an advisor, he or she must fashion a financial plan that meets your goals. If you are in your thirties and don't expect to access your savings or retirement for thirty years, you may very well be served by investing heavily in stocks. Likewise, if you are in your late sixties, you probably should be far more cautious and limit your exposure to market volatility.

For every prognosticator espousing doom and gloom there is one declaring the advent of the next bull market. What matters most is you and your money, and how you can successfully navigate whatever the market brings and still achieve your financial goals. It is absolutely possible to succeed with this priority, and the skilled advisor will take the time to listen to you, provide adequate measures to ensure against failure, and introduce you to asset classes that meet your expectations.

The Salesman

You can see this person a mile away—just way too slick for comfort. It's not his or her appearance but more their attitude. They act or recommend without fully understanding your needs. They want to move product and get commissions.

Let's talk a little about the lunch or dinner seminar. If the event is an educational review of general market conditions such as interest rates, the Federal Reserve's current decisions and how it may impact interest sensitive investments, the current fiscal disposition of Congress, and so forth, fine. But if it's a single-investment seminar designed to "sell" you a product, think twice. Years ago we would conduct limited partnership dinners to which clients and potential clients would be invited to dinner and a presentation. The seminar was designed to introduce an investment concept that may or may not fit an individual's portfolio. So far, so good, but the minute you feel any pressure to buy, put your checkbook back in your pocket—or better yet, leave it at home. You may have an interest in a variable universal life insurance (VUL) product and have been invited to attend a seminar that promises to explain a VUL in greater detail. It's a good occasion to learn, but please follow up your newfound information with a deliberate conversation with your trusted advisor.

Have you ever been invited to enjoy a "free" vacation? The single stipulation is that you must attend a forty-five-minute review of the advantages of owning a time-share. Most everyone who accepts this invitation says to themselves, "What harm? I won't buy, I'll just take my free three days at a resort." These seminars continue to be popular because they work. The sales staff is quite adept at presenting the many advantages to ownership. And the advantages are very compelling, effectively refuting each and every objection from the prospective buyer. Now, there are many people who really enjoy owning a time-share and find this an inexpensive and fun way to vacation. But the typical visitor is being sold, hopefully for the right reasons. Caution: Never go to a seminar not knowing the people who are sponsoring. This is where you are most likely to meet the slick, salesy person intent on one thing: sales!

The single most important method of determining salesy is simply sitting back and asking yourself, "Is this person listening to me and my concerns, or is he or she featuring this investment without understanding what

I need?" Picture yourself at an auto dealership. You have been introduced to a salesperson who tells you how lucky you are to be visiting today. "We have special financing today only." He quickly sizes you up and determines that you need a shiny new sports car, not knowing (or caring) that you have three children and a dog.

I would never begrudge any hard-working salesperson a comfortable lifestyle, but are there signs that might alert us to someone living beyond their means?

One of my earlier hires, an advisor who had a middle-class upbringing, wanted to play the role of successful businessman. He purchased a Mercedes, bought an expensive home in a gated neighborhood, and spent money that he didn't have. His only source of income was commission based. He was very aggressive and acted in his own best interests. Once it became obvious that he didn't have his clients' best interests at heart, I terminated him. One day later a competitor hired him because his production (commissions) were attractive to any company. No one bothered to call me to check why he was terminated. A year later, this second company fired him and he was barred from the industry, but not before he had taken financial advantage of several families. "Does the advisor care about me and my money more than he or she cares about their own income?" Carry this question with you as you consider your next financial move.

Run, Don't Walk

There are two conversations that you need to be especially wary of. The first is the advisor who recognizes that an investor has ample wealth and asks the client for a personal loan. It may seem innocent enough, but it is never appropriate. In fact, this is against the law and industry standards, and is specifically identified as an infraction unless it is fully disclosed to the advisor's firm. But even if it is disclosed, it is wrong. I don't care the reason. You are paying this person for advice. I would hope that the advisor is following his or her own advice and is succeeding financially. I submit that most advisors are paying attention to their own cash reserves and savings, and are certainly living within their means. But advisors are human and thus subject to human frailties. Consider Madoff's lifestyle. Most would classify his penchant for high living as nothing short of opulent, with homes in Manhattan and the Hamptons as well as a yacht and home in Palm Beach. Feeding the financial beast played a major role in his appetite and need for income. But Madoff didn't borrow, he simply stole. (He did ask his friend Carl Shapiro for a loan to bail him out, as noted earlier.)

The second conversation to be avoided is the one that asks you to consider an investment that is unregistered. In other words, the advisor's firm does not represent the investment. It might be a private equity opportunity in which someone is trying to raise capital to fund a real estate venture or some invention that will revolutionize the market. Of course, it's perfectly legal to invest as you see fit, but the implied or tacit approval from a registered representative is highly inappropriate and is against all firms' policies.

I recall an advisor who would meet with her clients in the company's conference room and pitch a real estate investment represented by a local attorney. The implication to potential buyers was that the advisor's firm was recommending this particular investment. Turns out that the attorney was selling the same property over and over again.

When he was found out he committed suicide and dozens of local investors lost their investments. Several sued the advisor's firm and won. The advisor, as you would expect, was terminated.

Understanding Your Advisor's Credentials

Registered Investment Advisor (RIA) or Broker Dealer (BD)?

In researching the differences between registered investment advisors and broker dealers, I ran across a statement from investorjunkie.com that read. "The reality is that, no matter whether you go with a RIA or a broker dealer, no one is going to look after your money as well as you will."[3] Truer words about investing have not been spoken. It is indeed important to understand the difference between these two very large groups of investing channels—but no one cares about your money more than you should.

A **registered investment advisor** is a person who has satisfied the qualifications to be registered with Securities and Exchange Commission (SEC). RIAs oftentimes work with higher-net-worth families, helping them to manage their wealth. Most often RIAs will assess a fee based on a percentage of the assets they manage (e.g., $2 million dollars at 1 percent would be $20,000 annually). Registered investment advisors have an important distinction from broker dealers. They are required by law to act as a fiduciary to clients. This means that the clients' benefit is the single most important consideration when making recommendations. Now, in reality, there are RIAs who subscribe to this mandate, and there are RIAs who act in their own best interest.

A **broker dealer** is someone who facilitates investment transactions. Like an RIA, broker dealers are expected to make suitable recommendations to clients. They are governed by the "prudent man rule" that states an appropriate recommendation is one that any prudent man would make. Larger broker dealers include Morgan Stanley, Wells Fargo, and Bank of America Merrill Lynch.

Perhaps one of the biggest differences is that RIAs' assets are "held away" at firms such as Fidelity and Schwab whereas broker dealers' assets are held within the firm. The same safeguards are applied to both channels, and regulation of each is actually very good. The SEC governs broker dealers and registered investment advisors with assets in excess of $100 million. For those with less than $100 million, RIAs are governed by the respective states.

There is a growing trend in the financial services business whereby traditional brokers, allied or employed by broker dealers, are leaving in favor of registered investment advisory firms, with many establishing their own. One criticism is that RIAs have less supervision than broker dealers. I suggest that the same number of Madoffs exist whether they are RIAs or BDs. This is further reason for personal due diligence—namely, yours.

So my former opinion is the best advice I can provide: *You* are the ultimate determiner to where you want to invest your money. It matters very little that your assets are with a registered investment advisor or broker dealer. What matters is the person with whom you are working, the confidence you have in their abilities, the level of trust they have demonstrated, and the competitive level of expenses that you incur annually.

In addition to RIAs and BDs, there are a number of individual designations that financial services individuals can attain. Following is a list of the most popular and also the most important.

Certified Financial Planner® (CFP)

In the spirit of full disclosure, your author is a Certified Financial Planner® and has completed extensive training through the College of Financial Planning in Denver, Colorado. I'm persuaded that financial professionals who successfully complete this regimen of study are serious about their chosen profession. The course of study can take two years or longer and challenges the aspiring candidate with a series of technically difficult exams culminating in a two-day "final" encompassing all aspects of financial planning. Upon completion, the advisor has the distinction of understanding most components of the planning process and probably far more than the non-CFP. The CFP certificant has studied the financial process, which includes financial planning, tax management, estate planning, insurance, risk management, and investments.

Does this mean that all CFPs are honest and competent? *No!* Does this mean that all non-CFPs are dishonest and not competent? *No!* But for some people in search of an advisor, it may be a good place to start looking.

Articles printed in noteworthy publications such as the *Wall St. Journal, Forbes,* and *Kiplinger's* will often reference the benefits of teaming with a CFP. And for good reason. It is the CFP's depth and breadth of knowledge and exposure to information that can be critical to a family's financial well-being. Before I continue to extol the virtues of education, let's recognize that there are several designations earned by advisors that help qualify the individual to provide excellent financial information.

Chartered Financial Analyst® (CFA)

This is a designation offered by the CFA Institute (formerly the Association for Investment Management and Research). To obtain the CFA charter, candidates must successfully complete three challenging exams and have at least three years of qualifying experience. Successful candidates will possess extensive knowledge in accounting, ethical standards, economics, portfolio management, and security analysis. This designation best serves individuals who buy and sell individual stock positions, as the specific training speaks to the many reasons why one buys and subsequently sells stocks. CFA designees tend to be analysts who work in the field of institutional management and stock analysis, not financial planning. They typically provide research and ratings on various types of investments. A traditional stockbroker or money manager is best advantaged by having the CFA certification.

Certified Fund Specialist (CFS)

There are literally thousands of mutual fund choices available to the investor. Individuals with this certification have demonstrated their expertise in mutual funds. They often advise their clients on which funds to invest in and, if they are properly licensed, buy and sell the investments on their client's behalf. The Institute of Certified Fund Specialists provides training for the CFS and the course focuses on a variety of mutual fund topics, including portfolio theory, dollar cost averaging, and annuity investment.

Chartered Financial Consultant (ChFC)

Financial advisors with the ChFC designation have demonstrated their comprehensive understanding of financial planning. The ChFC program is administered by the American College. In addition to successful completion of an exam in areas of financial planning, income tax, insurance, and investment and estate planning, candidates must have at least three years of experience in a financial planning capacity.

Chartered Investment Counselor (CIC)

Presented by the Investment Counsel Association, this designation is available to CFA charter holders who are currently registered investment advisors. The focus of this program is investment management. A typical CIC designee might manage large accounts and mutual funds.

Certified Investment Analyst (CIMA)

This designation focuses on asset allocation, ethics, due diligence, risk management, investment policy, and performance measurement. Individuals with a minimum of three years of industry experience who are investment consultants are eligible for this distinction. The Investment Management Consultants Association offers the CIMA coursework. Individuals who hold this designation are required to prove their expertise through continual recertification that requires CIMA designees to complete at least 40 hours of continuing education every two years. CIMA certificants tend to have careers with financial consulting firms, which involve extensive interaction with clients and the management of large sums of money.

Chartered Market Technician

To achieve this designation, individuals must pass three exams offered by the Market Technicians Association (MTA) and agree to adhere to the MTA code of ethics. Individuals with CMT designation have a demonstrated expertise in the field of technical analysis. Oftentimes, CMT will work for hedge funds and money management firms.

Certified Public Accountant (CPA)

CPAs have passed examinations on accounting and tax preparation, but their title does not indicate training in other areas of finance. Thus, CPAs who intend to gain expertise in financial planning and to legally engage in the investment arena typically become either a personal finance specialist (PFS) or CFP.

Chartered Life Underwriter (CLU)

This is a designation offered by the American College and is mostly held by individuals in the insurance business. The CLU designation is awarded to persons who complete a ten-course program of study and twenty hours of exams. The course covers the fundamentals of life and health insurance, pension planning, insurance law, income taxation, investments, financial and estate planning, and group benefits.

======

Even though advisors with these various credentials sound impressive, it is not enough to find a person with letters following his or her name and decide they must be okay. The very first step one should take is to simply go online to www.brokercheck.com. This is a website set up by the financial services industry (FINRA) and designed to alert investors to any infractions that an advisor may have. Having said that, infractions may be in the category of truly egregious or simply a nuisance complaint filed by an irate client. Even the most modest letter of complaint may wind up on an advisor's record.

You will find under "Disclosure Events" the following: "All individuals registered to sell securities or provide investment advice are required to disclose customer complaints and arbitrations, regulatory actions, employment terminations, bankruptcy filing and criminal or civil judicial proceedings." This will be followed by "Are there events disclosed about this broker?"[4] The answer should be *no,* giving you confidence to move forward with this individual for further consideration.

In fairness, there are advisors who unfortunately were wrongly accused of impropriety and have suffered the consequence of having a *yes* answer to the above question. In the event you find an advisor whom you are seriously considering and he or she has an infraction, you must ask that person about it. It could be as simple as the advisor was the subject of a complaint that was totally unfounded by the letter writer. Just as there are "rogue" advisors, there are "rogue" clients. FINRA reports all infractions for the consumer to consider.

On one occasion many years ago, I received a letter, as branch manager of a small office. The letter described one of the advisors in my office as acting without the consent of the clients. This proved to be totally false and was a source of embarrassment to an otherwise very honest man. There are many other false claims by clients as plaintiffs. Remember it only takes a letter of complaint to mar an otherwise clean record of professional service. If, however, there is more than one complaint against the advisor, you may want to continue your search for another advisor. If you see only one, my advice is to simply ask the advisor to explain the conditions surrounding his or her U-4 (the technical reference to an advisor's record).

CHAPTER 8

THE SEVEN FINANCIAL CONCEPTS YOU *MUST* UNDERSTAND

*"An investment in knowledge
pays the best interest."*
—Ben Franklin

It is not my intention to encourage you to become expert or even try to handle all aspects of financial management on your own. Rather if you can become conversant with the concepts and some of the language, it will become extremely advantageous. It will also have a profound effect on your trusted advisor, who will appreciate the fact that you are knowledgeable.

During my tenure as an advisor to hundreds of people, I quickly realized that most people simply handed the reins of their wealth over to me and trusted me to make the appropriate best choices for their future. Though indeed flattering and a little humbling, it is nonetheless an extreme responsibility. God help me if I made an error in judgment and lost principal in my client's accounts. Loss of principal (the amount one has invested) is part of the risk we all take when investing.

In my professional world I found it far more gratifying and helpful if I truly understood, not only the financial needs of a client, but also their emotional temperament. I encouraged the client to tell me their expectations. I needed each person to honestly describe how they might react if the market depreciated by 30 percent or even 40 percent as it did in 1987 and 2008, respectively. It's pretty easy for people to say, "Oh, I'd be okay with that because the market will come back, and it's just market value and not a true loss unless you sell." But the reality is that when faced with a seemingly out-of-control stock market and being reminded of this every moment of every day via the media, it's extremely difficult to remain calm.

One day in early 2009, near the bottom of the real estate and stock market bubble, I received a call from a client, a friend of mine who had reached her emotional tipping point. She had watched her million-dollar portfolio dwindle to about $600,000 and finally panicked. "Sell everything. I won't have anything left for retirement," she told me. In the financial world, this constitutes a "firm order," one that demands execution of the unsolicited trade. To do otherwise is a breach of all FINRA and SEC rules of good conduct. But I knew it was the absolute worst decision she could make. By selling everything, she would establish her loss, not just view lower market values on her statements.

I told her, as calmly as I could, "I know you're worried, but let's revisit your goals. We're saving for retirement, and these assets are an integral part of your retirement income plan. You have several years until you retire, and nothing has changed the quality of your investments other than current price." The stocks and mutual funds still paid dividends, still had earnings, and still held great longer-term investment advantage. "Sell everything," she insisted.

The call came to me about 1:00 p.m. I told her, "Mrs. S., please do me a favor. The market closes at 4:00 p.m. today. I'm asking you to think about your decision and if you still want to sell everything, please call me at 3:45 and I will honor your request." Three forty-five came and went without a call. In the following days, weeks, and months, the markets returned, and her full market value grew to exceed her previous valuation. Her retirement nest egg was preserved. Almost a decade later, I remember that conversation like it was yesterday.

Obviously, the value of a trusted advisor is critical to a family's financial success, but it's incumbent upon the client to actively engage in the process of planning. This demands that you have the ability to effectively communicate your intentions and to agree to the strategies. It is not our intent to become expert at all matters financial. But it is our intent to be conversant, so I am delivering information about several critical financial topics that I trust readers will be able to appreciate. Adherence to some very simple financial precepts has the capacity to help most people better control their emotions when it comes to financial decisions. In the case of Mrs. S., she had no logical reason to sell her portfolio, only an emotional one. When she further considered how well balanced her stock, fixed income, and cash reserves were, she was better equipped to make the right decision and not sell her retirement account.

1. The Importance of Cash Reserves

"Cash is king," or so goes the expression. In actuality, having cash or access to cash can be very liberating. When an opportunity arises, a person can respond immediately and is not dependent on borrowing or liquidating other asset classes.

Cash is defined as currency or immediate access to currency. It takes several forms, such as balances in one's checking account, savings accounts, money market funds, or short-term certificates of deposit, and even cash value of insurance policies. The level of cash available is personal and relative to one's comfort. Some people feel they need higher levels of savings or cash to meet short-term needs. A good friend and client of mine feels destitute if her cash reserves drop below $100,000. Even though her debt is almost nonexistent, and in my professional opinion her level of cash is far too high, I respect her feelings. After all, it is her money. Older Americans are typically more inclined to have larger cash reserves—a lesson learned perhaps as a result of their experiences in the 1930s. (I'm defining "older Americans" as people age sixty-five and older, who were raised in households that remembered the hardships of the 1930s.) I can't blame them. Many younger people just starting out may have far more modest savings. Their goals are significantly different from my friend who needs $100,000 in the bank.

According to a 1996 study by the Organization of Economic Cooperation and Development, between the years 1870 and 1930, American's savings rate, the percentage of our income we set aside for a rainy day, ranked first among the "big seven" industrial countries. This rate was measured as a share of net national product. Between 1960 and 1995, however, the American saver dropped from first to worst behind Japan, Germany, France, Italy, Canada, and the United Kingdom. Note that Japan and Germany, the two nations defeated in the Second World War, are among today's top savers.[1] The lessons of history are still fresh in their memories. Fortunes were lost in the wake of a destructive war waged between 1939 and 1945. Mind you, fortunes were made as well. The vast industrial complex that emerged as a result of America entering the war made many industrialists, investors and others, countless millions. All wealth is personal. There's an old saying: "A recession is when your neighbor is out of work. It's a depression when you're out of work." Never trust the government (or your advisor) to define your prosperity or financial comfort.

Cash can provide people with a great sense of security. The amount of cash that helps people feel that way varies greatly. An advisor may tell you that cash can be a risky asset class because inflation and taxes can readily eat up future purchasing power. The advisor is right, but there remains the emotional confidence that cash reserves provide.

It is no coincidence that the credit card began its ascent to cult status during the 1960s. Borrowing rapidly replaced savings as the principal method of purchasing goods and services. Immediate gratification is a powerful reinforcer. Young families who were saving for the future no longer had to. They could buy two family cars, a home, clothes, a vacation, and even groceries with a credit card. Saving money was so last generation.

The federal government inadvertently discourages savings by providing a tax deduction for mortgage interest expense (the amount of interest a homeowner pays to their lender each year). This is tacit approval from Uncle Sam that borrowing is good. A homeowner can borrow money up to the full value of his or her home and receive a reward from the IRS in the form of mortgage interest rate deduction. This single benefit is approval by the federal government that borrowing is good and savings unnecessary.

The minimum level of cash reserves that most Americans should consider is three months and ideally six months' worth of monthly expenses. Add up all your monthly financial obligations including rent or mortgage payment, insurance, food, utilities, clothing, entertainment, and so forth, and multiply by three. For instance:

Mortgage	$1,200
Auto Payment	400
Insurance	400
Food	500
Utilities/Phone	500
Clothing	150
Entertainment	250
Misc.	100
TOTAL	$3,500

So: $3,500 times three months is $10,500. Multiplied by six months, this equals $21,000. This ratio tells the saver that they should have somewhere between $10,500 and $21,000 in savings, money market, or some cash equivalent. These funds are to be used in an emergency situation. Maybe the roof needs to replaced, a new car is necessary, or the heat pump stopped working. Or maybe the chief breadwinner has lost his or her job. These cash reserves can cover a multiplicity of needs. The actual amount of money each person decides to keep in this capacity it determined by the individual or family. The aforementioned ratios are to serve as guidelines only. My friend needs $100,000, but you may feel comfortable with far less.

As we review cash reserves it's important to look at ratios.

Mortgage (or Rental Expense) Ratio

Housing expense, typically our largest expense and biggest lifetime investment, can be viewed in terms of ratio. Housing expense includes principal, interest, taxes, and insurance, referred to as PITI by lenders. A lender, mortgage broker, or bank looks at the borrower's income, usually over the past three years, to help determine how much the borrower is qualified to borrow. The ratio is typically 28 percent. In other words, a borrower can qualify for a loan if the annual payments are less than 28 percent of their household income. A family with gross income of $100,000 will qualify for a loan when the payments (PITI) are no more than $28,000 per year, or $2,333 per month. Remember: The lenders are in the business of lending. Their ratios are industry-accepted standards. They care more about making a securitized loan than your overall financial success. I submit that these ratios are inordinately high and all measures should be taken to minimize one's housing payment. What happens to the borrower when one of the two wage earners loses their job? Or one parent chooses to stay home with children? And could a certain percentage of the wage earner's discretionary income be better utilized in anticipation of the unexpected? Remember that taxes account for up to 50 percent of your gross income. Fifty percent for taxes and 28 percent for housing leaves you with about 22 percent to pay all the rest of your monthly bills, put the kids through college, take vacations, and save for the future.

Total Monthly Payment Ratio

Lenders ask you a lot of very personal questions for a reason. They work on probabilities. The probability of loan repayment is best when their ratios are in line. As I mentioned previously, they care very little about the borrower's success. Total payment ratio of all debt, housing, credit cards, auto loans, and so on is pegged at 36 percent. This means that the total of all one's monthly payments should be within 36 percent of the family's monthly gross income. Using this new ratio, the family is down to 14 percent of their income to devote to themselves (50% taxes + 36% debt repayment = 86%) And thus the government, the mortgage holder, and the credit card companies get paid first.

Is it any wonder that Americans do not (cannot) save enough money to steer clear of debt? No business can survive on revenue alone. Profit is necessary to expand and compete. Yet the average American family at the end of every month is left with no profit. They have failed to pay themselves first. If Americans are to survive and prosper financially, it is incumbent for them to view their personal households in terms of profit, savings, and growth. Budgeting, cash flows, cash reserves, debt reduction, and investment are critical to the survival of any business. Shouldn't these variables be an important part of the American family's pro forma? Paying attention to these two important ratios (housing and total monthly expense) is critical to the lender. But don't get fooled. As CEO of your family's business, stay well below these figures. By doing so you will have ample cash flow to build your wealth and, more importantly, establish your peace of mind.

Cash is a financial liberator. It provides the consumer with choices and leverage. The consumer has the advantage of negotiation. A debt-laden person is at the mercy of the marketplace, needing goods and services but unable to pay for them and thus resorting to credit. Credit is strictly on the merchandiser's terms and greatly increases the cost of any and all items purchased. Our goal is to generate discretionary income or positive and substantial cash flow.

I remain an advocate for the consumer, the very essence of this book. I try to keep a distance between the larger, macro conditions of the economy and focus on how consumers and taxpayers may advantage themselves in any environment. The question should never be "How's the economy?" It should always be "How's *your* economy?" To a large extent we can survive and prosper in most any economic condition if only we pay attention to a few constants. I've had the advantage of more than thirty years' experience in the financial services industry and an advanced certification, the CFP® designation, and yet the best advice I ever received was from an old preacher who told me two things: "Get out of debt and live within your means." Perhaps too simplistic but wise anyway. And as we are faced with so many complicated decisions, maybe we accept the wisdom of a learned man and build upon it.

One further note on real estate is important. In the not-so-distant past (2008), the real estate market took a terrible hit. People who were locked into mortgages, many of them adjustable rate, suddenly found themselves living in homes with a greatly depreciated value but still owing the former-agreed-upon valuation. Americans continue to have the gross misconception that real estate is a good investment. It might be, depending on when one buys and sells, but it also might be a terrible, illiquid asset class. It is only an asset class, much like owning shares of a company or an income investment. For many years real estate did indeed prove to be a great "investment," but this was largely due to demographics in the United States: More people, the so-called Baby Boomers, were maturing with families and needing housing. Builders and brokers couldn't find enough inventory, and that drove prices sky-high. Today the demographics are changing; Gen X-ers and Millennials are proving to be less interested in early marriage and family, and there are fewer of them.[2]

If you live in a home and own it, or are paying a mortgage, good for you. Please remember that you are making payments, not to sell your home at an inflated price years from today, but so that you have a home—a place to live. And that's just fine! But by all means, minimize the monthly expense if you can.

Permit me to issue a warning for the near future. The same people who juiced the mortgage markets starting with

Jimmy Carter's Community Reinvestment Act (designed to make it easy for all Americans to achieve the dream of home ownership) are at it again. Essentially, the much-vaunted CRA of 1977 lowered standards, thereby making it dishonestly possible for households who otherwise would not qualify for a mortgage loan to buy a house. Great concept, but the law of unintended consequences bankrupted hundreds of thousands of American families who simply couldn't pay their monthly principal and interest. And when you add the variable of unscrupulous lenders offering "teaser" rate loans knowing full well that the borrower would be unable to afford principal and interest in later years, you have the perfect storm for a housing bust.

Today, similar conditions exist not only in the housing market but also in the student loan market, subprime automobile lending, and the credit markets. A family can qualify for a home mortgage with no more than a 3 percent down payment. The debt both on a national and personal basis is at all time highs. Despite efforts by both major political parties to rein in debt, it continues to grow unabated. Traditionally, Republicans want to decrease spending while Democrats want to increase taxes. Unfortunately there may not be enough political will to do either. You and I can control our family debt and we simply must. Resist following the lead of our Uncle Sam; our ability to do so will greatly magnify our opportunity to lead a comfortable and assured lifestyle.

2. Insurance and Risk Management

Nobody likes to for pay insurance premiums, yet everybody needs insurance. But insurance expense has the capability of robbing a family of cash flow. All kinds of insurance should be evaluated but particularly life insurance. First of all, *you* don't need life insurance, your *family* does. A healthy approach is imperative when the need for insurance arises. My experience with financial matters has led me to believe that, in most cases, insurance should be purchased to protect the surviving members of a family when an income provider dies. The insurance industry markets a wide variety of products that blend insurance with investments or growth of cash values. These are called variable insurance policies or cash-value insurance policies, and there are many cases in which these policies are important. However, when trying to maximize cash flow to a household, I encourage clients to buy term insurance, so called because it protects the named insured's beneficiaries for a term of time, usually ten, fifteen, or twenty years. It is the least expensive form of life insurance and provides a death benefit to one's named beneficiaries free from taxation.

Term insurance is referred to as "use it or lose it" insurance. If you don't die within the time frame of the contract, you've paid the insurance company a lot of premiums and you have nothing to show for it—except your life! I'll take that bet and hope the insurance company wins. During my income-producing years and because my wife was also producing an income, we, of course, had good death benefit coverage. Our two incomes paid for our collective expenses and lifestyle choices. Sudden elimination of one of our incomes would create a financial hardship.

When we were younger and our children were in elementary school, my wife chose not to work outside the home. Even though as a stay-at-home parent she did not produce income, we carried term insurance on her life. The reason for this should be obvious. In the event a parent with young children predeceases their family, many expenses find their way into the household. Far beyond burial expenses, childcare, education, and housekeeping are just a few expenses that would have to be addressed. Many professional women or men, who decide to return to their careers when the children are in school, return to help fund future financial needs such as higher education for the kids and their own retirement. If a parent dies, these very real expenses continue to grow.

The question burning in everyone's mind is "How much death benefit insurance do I need?" The level of protection one needs is relative to lifestyle, debt, anticipated expenses (college funding), retirement of the surviving spouse, and general comfort. Perhaps an amount equal to eight times one's annual budget is a good place to start. If a family's annual budget, including taxes, savings, entertainment, and investment, as well as the normal monthly expenses of mortgage or rent, food, utilities, and insurance is, say, $90,000, and the breadwinner's income is $90,000, then a death benefit of $720,000 might be appropriate. The secondary breadwinner, or stay-at-home parent, might consider an amount half that much. Insurance is a personal consideration. When deciding how much is necessary, ask yourself, "What if . . .?"

When shopping for a term life policy, it is imperative to review the rating of the insurer. There are hundreds of insurance companies that would love to sell you coverage, but you should only purchase from the companies that enjoy the highest financial ratings. A.M. Best is a service that rates insurance companies' ability to make good on their promise of protection. Think of it: If you own a policy and need the benefit, you may only receive it if the company

is fiscally solvent. Fortunately the industry is highly regu-
lated, but it is incumbent upon the buyer to make certain
they are buying the highest quality from the most fiscally
fit companies. A rating of A+ or AA+ is most desirable.
Agencies such as Moody's Investor Service and Standard
and Poors also provide ratings. AAA from these services is
obviously considered the best. You can save money if you
buy from a lower-rated company, but you risk the company
not being able to pay your benefit in the event of a death.
Buy term and buy only from the highest-rated companies *if*
your primary reason for coverage is death benefit.

When I was in my early twenties I sold (or tried to
sell) accident insurance. I only lasted about a month, as
my heart really wasn't in it. I would knock on businesses'
doors, ask for the owner or manager, and pitch my product.
It went something like: "Hello, my name is Bill Francavilla.
May I have thirty seconds of your time? I'm representing
an accident plan that will cover you if you are injured or
killed while driving or riding in a car, bus, or truck. It costs
a modest $12 per month but will cover your incapacity or
death up to $10,000."

That's right, $12 per month. The sales force was
expected to make thirty calls per day, and the company
figured each successful agent would sell ten policies.
Some agents did. Your humble author did not. First of all,
insurance actuaries consider the law of large numbers to

compute risk and premiums. The law of large numbers absolutely worked in favor of the insurer because so few of the insured would actually ever need the coverage. And even at $12 per month, the company was hugely profitable. I don't begrudge a company from making money, but let's provide a fair and honest product or service with a fair price. More importantly, let's educate the ten people per agent per day with the requisite knowledge to make informed decisions. Maybe they really needed this type of coverage, but let's make certain it was necessary.

I remember hearing "I'm insurance poor" for the first time. So many people felt that their monthly premiums were sapping their cash flow. One should never have too much insurance, but certainly enough.

In addition to life insurance, there are probably three kinds of insurance that most Americans truly need: homeowners, auto, and health insurance. There are probably two more types of policies that Americans may need: disability and umbrella insurance.

Homeowners Insurance

If you have a mortgage, you have homeowners insurance. If you lose your insurance due to cancellation, your bank is notified, and they will provide you with insurance at your expense. If you don't have a mortgage, you need homeowners insurance. Fire, theft, flood, and so many other calamities can cause extreme financial hardship on a homeowner who doesn't have insurance. My wife and I recently had a pipe burst, which caused about $20,000 worth of damage to our first floor. Our homeowners insurance paid for all the repairs. I would rather not have monthly premiums, but I would absolutely rather have adequate coverage. You can minimize your premiums by adding security systems, bundling other coverages, and having a candid conversation with your insurance agent. They don't want to lose your business and may have some cost-savings ideas.

Automobile Insurance

All states require drivers to have adequate coverage. If you're uninsured and you get in an accident, your license will likely be suspended and you'll face a fine. Liability insurance is the least you need, and if your car is valued at more than $100, you need collision. Again, a candid conversation with a trusted agent (or two) is important. Notice how many property and casualty companies advertise on television claiming they can save you $400 or $500 dollars per year if you switch (to Geico, State Farm, etc.)? Shop rates with a reputable insurer and call their bluff.

Health Insurance

An appendectomy will cost $14,000 to $30,000; a baby's birth will cost $10,000 to $14,000; a hip replacement is $40,000 to $90,000, and the average hospital stay is $4,000 to $13,000 per day.[3] I know health insurance is expensive and President Obama tried to help with the Affordable Care Act, but the consequence of not having health insurance is far greater than a monthly premium.

If your profession is dependent on your direct participation, such as physician, dentist, attorney, sole proprietor, and many others, it is critical to have disability coverage. The likelihood of becoming disabled and thus out of work is far greater than needing death coverage. If a dentist, for instance, is injured and can't get to work, his or her income may dry up quickly. Here's where the disability coverage comes in. And you can tailor the policy to your needs. A key phrase is "elimination period." That determines the length of time you may be out of work before your benefit kicks in: the longer the elimination period, the less expensive the cost.

Umbrella Policy

This is like additional coverage to your homeowners and auto insurance. It's also very cost effective. If one exhausts his or her homeowners or auto benefit, the umbrella policy kicks in. People who have significant losses are most appreciative when they can use their umbrella policy. Also, people who have swimming pools or dogs might also think this is a good idea, as it comes behind traditional coverage.[4] A $1,000,000 policy may only cost $200 to $300 per year. You would buy this policy from your homeowners insurance agent.

3. The Ugly Nature of Debt

In 2017 the debt of the United States government topped $20 trillion. And yet few people seemed overly concerned. This debt is considered to be public debt. Total private debt, the amount owed by U.S. citizens, was $12.7 trillion. Mortgage debt, primary, and lines of credit attached to the homes equity were 71.4 percent. Student debt was the second largest private debt obligation at 10.9 percent, and auto loans were 9.2 percent. Credit card and other debt were

6 percent and 2.9 percent, respectively.[5] It's important to note that mortgage debt is typically a loan on a hopefully appreciating asset, one's home. Even though this is not a certainty, it has proven to be likely for most of the twentieth century. Student, auto, and all other debts are not attached to any appreciating asset and in your author's opinion may very well be very problematic in the decade to come. Bottom line is we are in uncharted territory having accumulated an unprecedented amount of both public and private debt.[6]

Too few people seem concerned. The financial pundits argue that debt is relative to income or assets. Yes, this is true, perhaps especially in the case of national debt. But unabated, debt will unwind even the most robust economy. Excessive debt has traditionally caused more recessions, depressions, and even wars throughout history. For any American who desires financial independence, reduction and eventual elimination of debt is tantamount to financial freedom.

After years in the financial services business I have come to appreciate the fact that the most relaxed, confident people are ones who have managed or eliminated their debt, no matter how great or small. I recall meeting a retired postal worker who was living on a modest retirement income and little investable assets. As he and I spoke he told me that he has zero debt (including his home), he spends less than his retirement income each month, and he and his wife enjoy life to its greatest extent. I could tell you that I've assisted families with far, far greater physical and tangible wealth and property, but I may never have met a more relaxed and contented couple than my postal retiree and his wife. What a joy—all because they had no debt. Of note is the fact that there are more verses in the Bible that refer to prosperity and wealth than any other topic, and it comes down to two principles: (1) Get out of debt, and (2) live within your means. Pretty simple.

Debt Reduction

In the history of the world there is no more certainty than that extreme debt is a prelude to extreme disappointment. We need only to consider the example of Germany following the First World War. The Versailles Treaty exacted extreme hardship on the German population. The victorious Allies demanded reparations from the German people, reparations that they could ill afford. The German government began a process known as monetization. They simply printed and printed and printed fiat currency (money backed by nothing more than the full faith and credit of the printing nation). This resulted in hyperinflation requiring employers to pay employees several times per day because the money printed in the morning was near worthless in the afternoon. A loaf of bread sold for millions of German franks. Monetization is a clever political solution to extreme debt. If you owe $100,000 on your thirty-year mortgage and inflation is 100 percent annually, you can ostensibly pay off your home in just a few years using the future value of money. What an insidious way to pay down debt because it also bankrupts the savings of the population. Everybody's broke. Anarchy typically follows; and in Germany's example, Hitler and the Nazis seized power. Desperate times force desperate people to do desperate things.

Personal debt is not only a financial burden but also a mental and emotional strain. According to psychologists, debt is the number one reason for divorce.[7] And yet, it can be managed. It takes discipline and determination more than income or resources. I've witnessed many examples of people who, faced with insolvency, make a decision to whittle their debt and live more confidently.

Budget

The first rule of debt reduction is to compose a simple budget, accounting for all monthly expenses including taxes. Leaving room for savings and reserve is critical. This is not a difficult assignment, but it is an important one. If you live alone, it should be easy; couples should do this together to include 100 percent of all expenses and income. If you find you are at a deficit each month, you've got a problem and must decide how to remedy. There will always be expenses that can be eliminated or at least minimized. I remember my mother admonishing younger people to spend less on coffee and put more in savings. Sage advice from a woman who lived to be eighty-seven and witnessed firsthand the Great Depression.

For a married couple a budget cannot be considered without 100-percent participation. The wife, for instance, cannot take full responsibility. I'm a strong proponent of joint checking accounts, savings accounts, investment accounts, and so on. I've seen far too many couples agree early on in their relationship to separate financial responsibilities: "You take care of the mortgage with your income, and I'll take care of the utilities and groceries with mine." Sounds equitable until one spouse loses his or her income. Money is not a contest, and marriage needs to be a partnership. It's like owning a restaurant where sales from beverages is earmarked for insurance while food sales go to rent and maintenance. It makes no sense.

If you are uncomfortable combining your household budget with your spouse, you are making it more difficult than it has to be. But if you insist, please be very honest and forthright with all income and expenses, and aggregate these figures so you can arrive at an honest budget. There are many sample household budgets available on the internet. Search "sample household budget" and choose a model that fits your comfort. Then fill in the blanks. You can readily see why it's critical to have both spouses participate. If you are single your task is actually a little easier because it's all up to you, both income and expenses.

One of the most challenging expenses is tax. Go to your pay stub and subtract your net income (income after taxes have been paid to the IRS, state, and locality) from your gross, and use this as the basis of income you have to pay the bills. I also suggest annualizing your monthly net income to take into consideration any real estate, personal property taxes as well as life and health insurances.

Most people can derive a pretty accurate picture after completing this task. Don't be surprised if there are several "a-ha" moments. This is truly financially introspective and exceedingly helpful. Any business that wants to grow must have a budget prepared and a profit-and-loss statement to determine if it can grow or if it should grow. If after a period there's more money coming in than going out perhaps the company might consider further expansion. A household budget is a collection of income and expenses, and it becomes a family's profit and loss. Can we afford to retire? Are the kids going to private or public schools? Can we justify a vacation in Europe? Unfortunately, most people make these decisions with no clear idea. This is dangerous, as one bad decision (e.g., funding college before considering retirement) might derail the overall comfort of a family.

Only following completion of this integral exercise can a family make intelligent decisions. And if you are in a negative position (more expenses than income) you can adjust. What can we do without? How might we generate more income? How can we eliminate our credit card debt? Years ago I took a course in debt elimination using a cascading method. For instance, a family is income neutral (income equals expenses) and they have several thousand dollars of debt spread over five credit cards. The solution can be pretty close at hand, as the following will demonstrate.

MasterCard: $1,500 owed, $40 minimum monthly payment

Visa: $575 owed, $15 minimum monthly payment

Lowes: $3,500 owed, $60 minimum monthly payment

Target: $100 owed, $10 minimum monthly payment

American Express: $7,500 owed, $100 minimum monthly payment

The family's total consumer debt is $12,975, and minimum monthly payments add up to $225. The smartest financial advisors will consider the percentage of interest each card charges and elect to pay the highest interest rates first. But I'm not the smartest. I am, however, the most logical and very experienced, so I say pay off Target first, Visa second, MasterCard third, Lowes next, and finally American Express. This gives a great feeling of accomplishment and reinforces a family's resolve. Forget about interest rates at this point and focus on debt elimination. This system works when the family has the cash flow to not only pay the minimum required but also to add as much as possible to the one targeted outstanding balance. So while paying the minimums on MasterCard, Visa, Lowes, and American Express, you are paying maximum on Target until it is completely paid off. Next you chip away at Visa, as it is the next lowest balance.

In order for this method to succeed, one must obviously make certain they have positive cash flow. If not, a more honest conversation must take place. What expenses can we minimize or eliminate? You've got to do this if you want to be successful. Otherwise don't bother reading the rest of this chapter.

Most families also have a lot of acquired (or assimilated) property. There are bikes and exercise machines that haven't been used in years. There might be lawn equipment or an extra freezer. Certainly clothes that are no longer worn. Sell them, sell them all, get rid of the clutter, and bring in some cash to pay down your debt. There are about 165,000 yard sales each week in America, and the total weekly revenue is over $4.2 million.[8] This is also somewhat redemptive about getting rid of your attic's ballast and clearing your space. My wife recently read *The Life-Changing Magic of Tidying Up* by Marie Kondo. She felt great satisfaction after reorganizing her belongings and eliminating junk we hadn't used in years.

In order to get out of this debt spiral, it's imperative to use credit sparingly. Once you've been successful at getting rid of the debt, you can be very selective about credit, using the most efficient cards and making certain that 100 percent of all debt is paid off monthly (with exception). For instance, if your credit score is higher, you will qualify for lower interest rates and better terms when borrowing becomes necessary. The reality is that most Americans don't have the luxury to buy an automobile or finance a college education with cash, so when it becomes necessary to borrow you'll have more competitive choices. Remember our discussion regarding cash reserves. It's important to have at least three months of expenses in a savings account to take care of emergencies and immediate need items.

My wife and I have chosen to have one "go-to" credit card to which we apply most all our purchases. We get airline tickets with our points and other modest perks, and most importantly we pay off the entire balance each and every month. Now I can use both my Target and Lowes credit card and receive a 5-percent discount on each purchase. I'm in. Anytime I can save money by being a little smarter, I take advantage. Also, our local supermarket provides a 5-percent discount for people fifty-five and older on Tuesdays and Thursdays. I love these savings. And I regularly shop at Walmart and Costco—not for entertainment value, but because their prices are better than the competition.

The bottom line is that even modest measures can provide huge benefits. One only has to think this process through and treat their household budget much like a business that must answer to shareholders (who are your family members).

4. The Wisdom of Investing According to Need (and Not Greed!)

The very first book I read on the securities industry was a Merrill Lynch publication that stated, "Everybody's an Investor." It matters little if they own stocks, bonds, real estate, or cash. People are constantly seeking out the best opportunities to protect or grow their wealth. In other words, even if a person has $1,000,000 in cash, he or she is an investor. That person believes, rightly or wrongly, that cash is the best "investment" for their situation.

Solutions-based financial planning is the single best way to approach investing. Just saying, "I want to grow my assets" is not enough because it lacks a specific outcome for your resources. It is much healthier to admit, "I need to save $40,000 for my child's college education in ten years." Ascribing a real event to a timetable brings considerable focus and accountability to the process. Likewise, when considering retirement, an absolute discipline must be adhered to so a proper plan can be effectuated. Permit me to begin with a review of what works and what doesn't.

I enjoy reading a wide variety of financial pundits and prognosticators. If I read ten different authors, I may get ten varying opinions, each one with a high degree of logic and believability. John Bogle of Vanguard Funds, once stated, "I don't know anyone who's got it right. In fact, I don't know anyone who knows anyone who's ever got it right."[9] Another reason Bogle is one of my heroes. He's honest and humble enough to admit the obvious: No one really knows what might happen in the financial markets. However, we all are compelled to make a decision. Do I think the markets are too high or fairly valued? Which mutual funds or companies do I think have the best opportunity for growth?

This is the precise reason I am a proponent for needs-based financial planning. Once a family or individual comes clean with realistic needs, they can then formulate a plan, not to get rich, but to meet their honest needs. Wealth may be a factor but too often the portfolio growth model gets in the way of meeting needs (need vs. greed!). Let's review what works.

Begin with a budget, get out of debt, and decide what goals are most important. This is a joint project for married couples. Is retirement more important than funding college? (Yes, in most cases, because parents may run out of time to fund their retirement years, and children have far more time to pay off their student loans and begin to build for retirement.) Long-term objectives need growth, and growth typically involves equities such as stocks or mutual funds. Over time, very, very few asset classes can compete with equities for growth.

Need for income means less growth and more bonds or dividend-yielding stocks. Sometimes income may be necessary to pay the bills today. Retired people find themselves in this position most often because they've essentially stopped working.

Anticipation for a financial event (large purchases, imminent college, overseas vacation, etc.) presents the investor with limited options, and the most obvious option is to have a large cash reserve (one that goes beyond three or six months of expenses). I recall during one period of rapidly accelerating stock market prices that a realtor friend of mine would take the proceeds from one successful home sale, plow it into a no-load fund, and take it out when he needed the cash for another real estate purchase. It worked until October 1987, when his "savings" was cut by a third in one day. Not a good plan and certainly not needs based.

Some of the reality checks that we all must face include the fact that even though most people think they can handle volatility and can quickly make the decision to get out of the market, they can't. Markets move too quickly and when the stock market rapidly declines, most people will not sell until it's down precipitously. *Morningstar* published the findings of a study that sheds considerable light on the market timing mentality. They found that between 1995 and 2014 if an investor missed the ten best days of performance, their returns would be reduced from 9.9 percent per year to 6.1 percent. If one missed the top-twenty best days of market performance during the same period, the return would be reduced to 3.6 percent.[10] Please don't delude yourself by believing you know when those top (and bottom) days and periods will take place; you don't know and neither does anyone else.

Sticking with one mutual fund or stock may be a great strategy. But please let me encourage the reader to monitor closely not only the securities performance but also any change in management or management style. Different funds with different objectives behave differently in various market cycles. Also, even the best performing companies in particular industries will perform quite differently when economics change. Witness some of the most rock-solid energy companies like Exxon Mobil and British Petroleum when the price of oil went from $100 per barrel to less than $40 in 2015–2016. The market woke up to the fact that there was way too much oil and not enough demand.

Or consider the performance of legendary fund manager Bill Miller, who beat the S&P 500 Index for fifteen straight years during the 1980s and 1990s. I knew Bill, as he was a superstar with my former company, Legg Mason. Our investors were very gratified and financially rewarded by remaining invested in Bill's Value Trust during that time. And then he stumbled, and the value of people's portfolios stumbled as well.[11] No one is impervious to making bad choices, not even Bill Miller.

What about the discussion about index funds and actively managed funds? Index investing is simply buying an index, like the Standard and Poor's 500, and active management is selecting a fund designed to outperform the index. In this case the fund manager makes deliberate decisions as he or she sees the market. Is one better than the other? The answer is determined by several variables: How long will the monies be allowed to grow? Will the owner have a need for the money anytime soon? Can the owner handle the emotional roller coaster that invariably will ensue? I recently advised a relative of mine to purchase a Vanguard S&P 500 Index fund and add a set amount to the fund each month. Why? Because my cousin is twenty-five years old and has no need for the money and is long-term-oriented. He's also quite mature and understands that there will be disappointments with the markets (thus the reason we dollar cost average each month by putting a little money into the fund).

I also advised an older couple who just might have a need for income or even principal distribution in the not-too-distant future to own a balanced portfolio that is professionally managed. These people have little understanding of macroeconomics and would be very upset if their portfolio went down precipitously. It just depends on a client's age and circumstances.

I trust this review and discussion is helpful as I am trying to convey the very honest and very personal decisions that we all must make as responsible guardians of our wealth. I hope readers realize that a lot of people just might be capable of designing their own financial plan and possess the temperament to stick with it. My experience tells me that these people are in the minority and that most people are better served by an honest and proficient financial advisor. This discussion is just that: a discussion. In no way do I expect this work to be a book on comprehensive financial planning, rather this is a book on avoiding disappointments.

5. The Prudence of Minimizing Taxes

This is pretty big. Most Americans don't realize that 50 percent of their salaries and wages is taken by various taxing authorities: income tax, capital gains tax, property tax, sales tax, personal property tax, lottery ticket purchases (commonly referred to as the poor man's tax), gas tax, and so on. It should be every American's responsibility to try to minimize his or her tax burden for family reasons and also for patriotic reasons. Every dime the government receives, it spends—and then some. (Note the federal debt of $20 trillion!)[12] And there are measures that we can take to legally accomplish this important initiative.

First a quick review of the six most prevalent ways Americans pay taxes. By some estimates there are up to 100 ways various taxing authorities tax their constituents.

Income Tax

Income tax was considered unconstitutional until 1913. It took an amendment for the federal government to initiate a tax on income. Income tax can be collected by individual states and localities as well. Relative to the federal income tax, there are currently seven brackets. For each additional dollar in a new bracket, the taxpayer pays the new tax rate. States vary widely. Florida assesses no income tax, and California has a very steep income rate, topping 13 percent.

Sales Sax

This across-the-board tax is levied irrespective of income bracket. It is a percentage of the goods or services purchased. Tennessee has the highest sales tax in America (9.44 percent). Alaska, Montana, New Hampshire, Delaware, and Oregon have no sales tax.

Payroll Tax

Employers and employees alike pay Social Security and Medicare taxes that are subtracted from each paycheck. Social Security takes 6.2 percent and employers must match that for a total of 12.4 percent. Likewise, Medicare takes 1.45 percent from both employee and employer to total 2.9 percent. (People earning more than $200,000 chip in an extra .9 percent.)

Property Tax

Every state collects property taxes, but they vary widely. Hawaii has the distinction of the lowest effective real estate tax rate at .28 percent. (A $500,000 home has an annual tax assessment of about $1,400.) Typically there is a local tax based on a homeowner's property valuation. Some locales or states will also tax personal property such as automobiles, boats, or other vehicles.

Excise Tax

Similar to a sales tax, an excise tax is charged on certain items. It is sometimes referred to as a sin tax and includes such items as fuel, diesel fuel, and tanning services. The federal government also collects such taxes, including 18.4 cents per gallon on gasoline and 24.4 cents per gallon on diesel fuel.

Estate Tax

Fifteen states have either an estate or inheritance tax, some both. As of 2018, if your estate was valued at more than $5.6 million (11.2 million for married couples), your estate is subject to federal tax at your death. The federal tax can run as high as 40 percent, and some states impose their own estate tax. Estate valuation includes cash reserves, securities, insurance, real estate, personal property, collectibles, and so forth. This tax has been subject to much criticism and is a political football. Most estates have to be settled within nine months of the deceased death. Consider the landowner or farmer whose family has to sell the $10 million farm to pay the estate tax.

———

Of course there are other taxes—far too many to list (lottery, gift tax, etc.)—but trust me when I say that our tax rate is close to 50 percent.

Being mindful of taxes is critical. Once you've paid a tax, that money is gone forever. When you consider that it can be as high as 50 percent of your income, one must take measures to minimize this burden in a very proactive manner.

I believe strongly in the value of solid, objective advice. I never intend to defraud the government of its legal access to taxes, but I certainly don't want to pay more than I am legally obligated. A trusted Certified Public Accountant and a good financial advisor who is schooled in tax minimization strategies are always welcome to advise and recommend amendments to my portfolio. These are dollars well spent. If you're so inclined and want to minimize sales, property, and estate taxes, you might consider living in Hawaii, working in Florida, shopping in New Hampshire, and dying in Virginia, where there is no estate tax. Absent that possibility, get an accountant and double-check his or her tax planning with another accountant. It's perfectly acceptable to shop professionals.

6. The Necessity of Estate Planning

If you care about your family, you will have a will. I can't say it any plainer. Dying intestate (without a will) is just lazy. You've abdicated your responsibilities to the state to make decisions for you because that's what will happen. It's expensive and so unnecessary.

I'm like you: I think naïvely that I'm going to live forever, or at least for much longer. But years ago my wife and I enlisted the support and professional assistance of a capable attorney who listened to our needs and wishes, and drafted our revocable living trust accordingly. When Rita and I depart this earth, I hope there are assets left to financially enable our children and grandchildren. In essence we've built a legacy. I recall the funeral of a dear friend and client. Her granddaughter, still in high school, eulogized her grandmother, saying, "Grandma loved me all my life, and her life and legacy live, due to her thoughtful generosity to me and my sister."

I recall another client who was in his eighties and had no will. When I asked him and his wife why, they became uncomfortable. Knowing the importance of this document, one afternoon I invited them into my office and, with neither their knowledge nor permission, I contacted their attorney, a friend of mine. I had set up this appointment beforehand and hoped they would agree. They did, and we drove to Alvin's office. What Alvin or I didn't know was that they had a daughter who was somewhat of a renegade, and they simply didn't want to deal with the thought of her receiving any inheritance. The emotional pain of an estranged child convinced them that it was better off to take no action at all. Upon uncovering this information, we were able to help them with their nearly $3 million estate. They chose to fund a charitable trust, enriching two of their favorite charities. Had they not taken this action, their daughter, regardless of the painful estrangement, would be entitled by state law to the full amount of inheritance. Another family had a special needs child that they feared would go uncared for upon their deaths or infirmities. I suggested a special needs trust that would be funded for the eventuality of their predeceasing the child.

What about a couple, both of whom have been married before and both with children from previous marriages? This is very common. It also presents special considerations that need to be vetted and agreed upon. Who gets what? What's fair? Tough questions but critical questions to answer. We won't live forever, and neither will our children or grandchildren, but we can have a positive and lasting impact on our loved ones with a simple gesture. My advice is to see a lawyer and get it done. You can do this by yourself with an online service such as legalzoom.com and for some people this may very well suffice. A better choice may be to seek the assistance of a qualified attorney to make suggestions to you and your family that you may not have considered.

7. Truly Enjoying Retirement

There are at least two discussions about retirement: retirement as a socioeconomic event and "my" retirement.

Retirement as a Socioeconomic Event

The concept of retirement is actually rather recent, less than 140 years old. It was Otto von Bismarck, the president of Prussia, who in 1881 suggested that there might be some benefit to helping Prussians in their old age. Von Bismarck was being pressured by liberal elements in his country to do something for the people in his country. He created a retirement system that provided for citizens over the age of seventy. The typical life expectancy for people in Prussia at that time was far less than seventy. Before this was enacted, people would just keep working for as long as they physically were able.

In the 1920s some American industries were promising pensions pegged to age sixty-five. And then in 1935, the Social Security Act was passed. Life expectancy for the average American was fifty-eight. Life expectancy for American men today is about seventy-six, and for women it's about eighty-one.[13] There are presently 10,000 Americans retiring every day.[14] One need not be a mathematician to quickly figure out that the math doesn't work. Each year there are fewer working Americans supporting more retirees. This is due to the massive number of people born between 1946 and 1964, the so-called Baby Boomers. The unfunded debt, when considering both Social Security and Medicare obligations, swells our total debt to over $100 trillion (from about $20 trillion today). Unless Congress addresses this quickly and directly, our country will be in a world of financial hardship.

"My" Retirement

When asked what the most pressing financial goal is, most Americans indicate that saving for retirement is first and foremost according to a survey conducted by Prudential Investments.[15] This same survey also indicated that Americans give themselves a solid "C" relative to their efforts. The survey went on to uncover that 66 percent of Americans think investing is complex and confusing and 43 percent are not knowledgeable about the types of products they have invested in; 74 percent think they should be doing more to become prepared, and 40 percent have no idea what to do. Though 24 percent think they will need $1 million to fund their retirement, 54 percent of pre-retirees have less than $150,000 saved. My insistence on minimizing and hopefully eliminating debt is strong. We truly cannot predict what the overall economy will bring, but we can predict with certainty that if a family has little or no debt, they will be advantaged during retirement.

Remember my older postal employee? He's the one who reminded me that being debt free and living within one's means are the only two variables necessary for a comfortable retirement. So how about magnifying this simple solution and customizing it to meet your retirement needs? What if you retired with no debt; had ample savings, retirement income, and other resources; and spent less than you earned each month? Would that constitute a comfortable lifestyle, however interpreted?

Here's where the previous six factors contributing to financial well-being play an important role. Savings, risk management, elimination of debt, carefully considered asset allocation relative to your needs and comfort, minimization of taxes, and proper estate planning all play an important role. By taking care of the details and by all means avoiding being scammed, the prospect for a successful and comfortable retirement is certainly within most people's reach.

Should retiring Americans downsize their home? Should they take another job or consult? How should older people occupy their time during the day? Do these people move to a state that takes a smaller percentage of income tax or estate tax? Do these people have ample savings or insurance for when and if they need further custodial care? Do they move closer to children or grandchildren?

Each of these questions is very important to the soon-to-be or retired American. And only that person can best answer. A financial advisor may make recommendations as to how best to make certain wealth outlive the investor, but it is the person himself or herself who best determines what fits in their life.

CHAPTER 9

THE THREE FACELESS MADOFFS

*"The function of economic forecasting is
to make astrology look respectable."*
—John Kenneth Galbraith

It has been my intent to identify people in the market-place that act contrary to your best interest. We've looked at famous, infamous, and Madoffs next door in an effort to be alert and diligent. It's quite improbable that upon reading this book you will be 100 percent prepared to recognize 100 percent of potential scams. But a healthy dose of skepticism coupled with a thorough appreciation for the twin towers of deceit (subtlety and naïveté) will make it far more difficult for people to steal your wealth.

As if remaining vigilant at all times isn't enough, permit me to introduce conditions that have historically robbed people of their possessions. They are the faceless Madoffs, and they are as nefarious as criminals. They are **inflation, deflation,** and **geopolitical events**.

We've all heard these three terms bantered about, and at some level there is a degree of complacency, especially among Americans. I say this because when we hear or read about hyperinflation in post–First World War Germany, or three decades of deflation in Japan, or certainly wars or vast population dissent that destroy nations, we say, "That could never happen here."

I get it. I hope that these faceless Madoffs never make it to our shores, but it's naïve to believe we are impervious to such conditions. Inflation, deflation, and geopolitical events qualify for susceptibility to both naïveté and subtlety, and as such must be respected. I've heard people say, "Well, in that case we'll all be in the same boat, so it doesn't matter." How foolish and irresponsible. I believe by paying attention not only to people but also conditions we can greatly minimize the possibility of being caught financially flat-footed. And there are measures that ordinary Americans can take to stay ahead of the masses that might encounter a large-scale financial catastrophe.

I love John Kenneth Galbraith's quote, "The function of economic forecasting is to make astrology look respectable."[1] It concisely and honestly presents what should be the obvious. Financial soothsaying is *not* available. Can we and should we stay sensitive to conditions that can impact our wealth? Absolutely. And this is strongly encouraged and should be the domain of not only the so-called experts but also the person it impacts the most: you. You don't have to be an expert, merely a pragmatist. A friend of mine, a Naval Academy graduate who spent several years in the Marine Corps, told me that his military training taught him to be aware of one's environment at all times. When he enters a restaurant, he looks around. Is there anything unusual, or are there any people who catch his attention? You and I should act likewise. What is going on in the financial markets? How might this impact my family and me? Joseph Kennedy in the late 1920s pulled all his money out of the stock market when the guy shining his shoes told Kennedy that he was "all in" the stock market because the market was going to go higher. This is akin to the tech bubble of 2000, when it seemed everybody was taking advantage of free money. One only had to buy a technology stock and watch it grow to the moon.

In Kennedy's case—and because he was aware of his surroundings—he made a family fortune that lasts to this day. (He wisely reinvested following the market crash of 1929–1932.) And the millions of Americans who greedily thought they could make a similar fortune during the early 2000s by buying technology, lost their investments. What was the major difference between Joseph Kennedy and most Americans? Kennedy was contrarian because he was able to discern what was occurring in the financial climate of America. He went against the grain. This is tough to do because emotionally, it hurts. And let's add two more gems of financial wisdom. Benjamin Graham, the father of value investing famously quipped, "Individuals who cannot master their emotions are ill-suited to profit from the investment process."[2] And one further comment worthy of our discussion is from Shelby Cullom Davis, founder of the Davis family of mutual funds who reminded us, "You make most of your money in a bear market, you just don't realize it at the time."[3]

Wow, if we could divorce ourselves from emotions and embrace the wisdom of people who have had the intestinal fortitude to do so, we would be a lot wealthier than we are.

As I previously mentioned, on October 19, 1987, I was in my office in Williamsburg, Virginia, conducting normal business on behalf of my clients and friends when the market took a terrible turn. It dropped by a third that day and in the days that followed. We were so busy simply responding to incoming calls from frantic investors that we were literally unable to make any outgoing calls. Obviously there was a major sell-off of all stocks. The sky was falling. While I hope I was able to convince most people not to sell, quite a number decided to submit to fear. And once an investor submits to fear (or greed), the person is no longer an investor. He or she is merely a market participant subject to the folly of emotion.

The three faceless Madoffs—inflation, deflation, and geopolitical events—are conditions that can take place without fanfare, and because most of us are naïve and because these conditions can be subtle, we succumb. We are talking about the virtual value of capital—money. Though investments and the cash we have in the bank have a daily relative value typically assigned to markets or other currencies, it's important to think of money in terms of being an asset. Cash is indeed an asset, but what that cash can purchase is subject to how much the cash is actually worth.

Our three faceless robbers of wealth bring a new dimension to our discussion of protecting your wealth, family, and well-being. Nonetheless they must be considered even though they may be outliers. Before we address these issues let's make sure we understand the difference between monetary and fiscal policies of the United States, as they both deal with the value of money.

Monetary Policy

We often hear the chair of the Federal Reserve or a newscaster referring to the "monetary policy" of the Fed. Policy has to do with the direction of employment and inflation and how interest rates should respond. If unemployment is high, for instance, the Fed may decide to lower interest rates and help employers borrow money to expand their businesses, and thus hire more employees. If inflation is high, the Fed may decide to raise interest rates to slow the economy until prices are more stable. Paul Volcker, the Fed chairman in the early 1980s, was a fierce opponent of inflation and raised rates to modern history heights. (I was personally borrowing money at 20 percent to finance a project, one that failed because I couldn't make the debt payments.) The Federal Reserve has extreme autonomy, and its impact is huge.

The Federal Reserve, its governors, and especially its chair (Jerome Powell at the time of this writing) wield extraordinary powers. If their data is interpreted correctly, they can indeed provide guidance to the economic prosperity of the nation. If, however, their data is incorrect and they direct interest rates in the wrong direction, the results will be felt almost immediately and may last for several years. The stock market will take its cue from the statements of the chair. If the Fed chair intimates that rates may have to go higher, we might see a sell-off in the stock market. Even though this could be deemed best for the overall economy, the market or holders of stock may interpret this as being a catalyst for a slower economy. Slower economic conditions don't necessarily portend well for holders of stock.

The Federal Reserve is not a branch of the federal government. It was established in 1913 in an effort to smooth markets, maintain sustainable employment, and control inflation. It continues to be controversial because, since its inception and in spite of its efforts, the United States has experienced tumultuous markets, record high unemployment, and staggering inflation. There have been initiatives to disband the Federal Reserve, all with no real results. Central bankers have always been controversial. I'm of the opinion that markets should decide interest rate levels. If there is demand for money based on true economic growth, then rates should indeed be higher—and would be because of supply and demand. In his book, *The Signal and the Noise: Why So Many Predictions Fail—But Some Don't,* Nate Silver interviewed Jan Hatzius, the chief economist of Goldman Sachs, to find out why so many economic predictions miss the mark. "Nobody has a clue," Hatzius told Silver. "It's hugely difficult to forecast the business cycle. Understanding an organism as complex as the economy is very hard."[4]

Please recall that John Law, one of our infamous five, was dead wrong with his prognostications and solutions. His decisions as a central banker were dead wrong, and perhaps more significantly, the ranking officials and people of France believed him. Law, the charming salesman, died

disgraced and penniless, and the investors in his national-
ized scheme of monetary policy lost fortunes.

Fiscal Policy

Fiscal policy is the domain of Congress and the president.
Our elected officials decide the federal budget and how
best to pay for it. Congress plays a critical role in the health
of our economy. When legislation raises or lowers taxes, it
has an impact on not only the mood of business owners
and corporations but also profitability. In December 2017,
when President Trump signed his tax bill into law, the
stock market surged ahead anticipating economic growth
and expansion.

In times of economic duress, it seems logical that
Congress should lower the tax base on taxpayers and businesses, thus stimulating investment and spending. There
are diverse opinions among our representatives on just
how to best stimulate an otherwise languishing economy.
Some suggest that the best way to attain prosperity is to
spend your way by hiring more government employees
and fostering government programs that will hire more
Americans. This suggested solution requires either higher
taxes or higher deficits (or both). The short run may produce the desired results, but the longer term has to deal
with perhaps more debt and maybe even the exact opposite of what was intended. We've seen periods when unemployment, debt, and taxes were all high. Again, this is an
attempt to manage, massage, and even legislate financial
well-being. It just doesn't work this way. The markets need
to be free to allow the principal of supply and demand to

meet the needs of the people. This includes interest rates as well as the availability of affordable goods and services.

Both monetary and fiscal policies are widely debated and very controversial. But they are a reality, and they matter. It is always important to consider the propensity of a current Congress and president as well as the Federal Reserve's chair and members.

=====

Now let's consider the three faceless Madoffs: inflation, deflation, and geopolitical events. The basis of wealth is money or the fiat use of money. Fiat is using our dollars and checking accounts to buy goods and services. There is no value in fiat money other than what it represents, namely, the amount of money at current valuations. If, for instance, the U.S. dollar is priced favorably against foreign currencies, people who make purchases with the dollar can buy more from Canada, Japan, and other countries. I have a friend who worked in Canada for several years and bought all his suits and shoes in Canada using American dollars. The Canadian dollar was trading at a discount to the U.S. dollar, and he could buy anything Canadian for a 35 percent discount. Smart. But the U.S. dollar does not always trade at a premium to other currencies, and this is the result of fiscal and monetary policies.

So when we think of the value of money, let's look at what inflation does to your wealth. In a word, it destroys your wealth. Paul Volcker knew this, and he raised rates until inflation was subdued.

Inflation

Historically speaking, no discussion of inflation would be complete without referencing Germany following the First World War. Germany lost the war and was compelled to pay reparations to the victors. This was impossible as Germany was broke. The Weimer Republic decided it would pay the Allies by borrowing money. The Versailles Accord demanded that Germany pay for the Allies' losses incurred between 1914 through 1918. The German people could ill afford to be taxed, so borrowing was the only solution. At its worst in October 1923, the monthly inflation rate reached 29,500 percent. The exchange rate of marks to dollars was 4.2 trillion to one.[5] German workers were paid several times per day because the value of the mark in the morning was much less than the afternoon. Germans began using the worthless currency as a substitute for firewood and coal because it was cheaper. There are numerous photos and stories attesting to ordinary Germans carting wheelbarrows full of cash to the grocery store to purchase a loaf of bread. This terrible financial burden on Germany led to political upheaval and the eventual rise of the National Socialist Party, with Adolf Hitler at its head. History does repeat itself, and the consequence of monetary valuation can never be minimized.

Between 2000 and 2009 Zimbabwe's annual inflation rate stood at 516 quintillion percent. At one point the Zimbabwean treasury printed a 100-trillion-dollar bill so citizens didn't have to lug around a boatload of cash.[6] President Mugabe's domestic policies of extremely excessive spending financed by the reserve Bank of Zimbabwe were the exact cause of this hyperinflationary condition. A few paragraphs ago we learned of the power of central banks. This stands out as a prime example of wrong decisions designed to fuel a fabricated prosperity. Mugabe blamed the United States and European Union sanctions for the economic chaos.

How about Argentina in the 1980s? In 1992 the overall inflation resulted in one peso being equal to 100 billion pre-1983 pesos.[7] Argentina's inflation stemmed from heavy external borrowing, and when they could no longer borrow money from foreign countries, they devalued the peso to increase its trade surplus.

The result in each of these three countries was abject poverty for people who held the German mark, Zimbabwean dollar, and Argentine peso. Their currencies could buy nothing. But it could never happen here, right? According to the U.S. Inflation Calculator (usinflation calculator.com), since 1913 and the inauguration of the Federal Reserve, 10 percent annual inflation has taken place ten times. Nowhere near as dangerous as hyperinflation that is typically defined as annual inflation greater than 50 percent, but nonetheless destructive. In 1917 inflation was pegged at 17.4 percent; in 1918 it was 18 percent; and in 1919, 14.6 percent. During that cumulative three-year period, the U.S. dollar was worth about 50 percent less than it was in 1913. The First World War indeed took its toll on our economy as well. Additionally, 1920 saw 15.6 percent. In 1974 the U.S. inflation rate was 11 percent. Anybody remember Gerald Ford sporting his "Whip Inflation Now" (WIN) button? It took more than a button. Painful personal remembrance of inflation at 13.5 percent in 1980 still haunts me.

Inflation will occur when a government either spends or borrows too much. Today we run annual budget deficits that economists always measure against gross domestic product (GDP) of the United States. The GDP is the sum of all money spent in the country, and if the ratio is modest, the same economists will suggest that the economy is healthy. This ratio does not take into account the excessive debt that our country has on its balance sheet. The federal debt as of this writing is about $20 trillion, but if one considers unfunded liabilities such as Social Security and Medicare, the debt swells to over $100 trillion.[8] Who wants to lend money to a nation with those financials? I believe that if we don't address both the deficit and debt, it will lead to further and perhaps exacerbated inflation in the years to come.

Deflation

The ugly cousin of inflation is deflation. It is the exact opposite, as money is highly valued but goods and services deflate in value. It sounds like it's a good thing for consumers, but it really isn't because the value of all property, real estate, and stocks depreciate, resulting in lower borrowing authority among business people. Lower creditworthiness means banks are not willing to lend. Additionally, what bank wants to lend money with no return? The United States has experienced five years of deflation since 1913: In 1921 deflation was at 10.5 percent, and from 1931 through 1933, deflation rates were 9, 9.9, and 5.1 percent, respectively.[9]

We need only to consider Japan, once the shining star of innovation, productivity, and manufacturing. Since 1992 deflation has been a fact of economic life. In 1996 the average wage for a Japanese worker was Y315,000. In 2015 the average was Y289,000. During this same period, food in the United States has inflated 66 percent, whereas in Japan, only 9 percent. Housing in the United States is up 60 percent, and in Japan it has appreciated 2 percent.[10] At first glance one might consider this to be a good thing. But it's not. When you factor in wage growth or lack thereof, it means that Japanese consumers, businesses, and lifestyles have suffered considerably. Deflation results in lower job security, anemic wage increases (or decreases), and a lackluster attitude toward consumption.

One of the principal causes of deflation is an aging population. The Japanese are a decade ahead of America with their rendition of Baby Boomers. Within the next several years a full 76 million Americans born between 1946 and 1964 will be fully retired.[11] Retirees spend a lot less than people who are employed, and this alone could lead to a period of deflationary pressures here at home.

Geopolitical Events

Our final faceless Madoff is the geopolitical events that take place almost daily. Most have no or only modest impact on markets and currencies, but every several years an event of magnitude takes place, usually by surprise, that significantly impacts markets and wealth. The clearest most recent example took place on September 11, 2001, when the United States was attacked by radical Islamist terrorists, most of whom were from Saudi Arabia, our alleged ally.

In the days and indeed years following the downing of the World Trade Center Towers and damage to our Pentagon, the financial markets reacted in dramatic context. The stock market closed for four trading days, the first time since the Great Depression, when FDR declared a two-day bank holiday to prevent a run on the banks. The markets reopened on September 17 when the Dow Jones promptly fell 7.13 percent.[12] The attacks also aggravated the 2001 recession contracting the economy by 1.3 percent in the third quarter of 2001.[13] Further, there were threats of war as President Bush declared a war on terror and told Americans it would be a lengthy campaign.

Perhaps the biggest economic impact was the debt crisis that resulted from the United States increasing the debt by over 11 percent ($1.8 trillion) to wage war in Afghanistan and Iraq.[14] High debt levels became a real crisis in 2011, ten years after the attacks when Treasury Secretary Paulson declared an emergency of confidence and cash. All this from a single geopolitical event by a mob of fanatics. Geopolitical events are omnipresent. How would people, markets, and currencies react to North Korea or Iran detonating a nuclear bomb or, worse, using it against an avowed enemy (us)? How might the world respond if Pakistan attacks India or Russia decides to occupy Ukraine? If a dirty bomb or electromagnetic bomb with capacity to destroy a country's ability to access its power grid or banking system? The results would be catastrophic.

When one of these three faceless Madoffs strikes, there is little we can do to protect our purchasing power or currency. We can, however, decide to own a "store of value" capable of maintaining our ability to trade, barter, or purchase basic necessities. This commodity is time honored and exceedingly effective. It is gold. From the earliest records of history, gold has always occupied a special distinction. Because of its relative rarity, luster, and ability to be smelt into a variety of uses, gold is a very special and distinct novelty. Gold is not a good investment. It doesn't pay a dividend, doesn't earn money like a corporation, and so floats in value principally because of inflation, deflation, and geopolitical variables. Gold is an excellent hedge and in times of need can be extremely important to own. Together with other commodities like silver, food, and water sources, as well as precious jewels or collectibles, it should be considered as an auxiliary to an otherwise-balanced investment portfolio.

Many financial advisors agree that perhaps 5 to 10 percent of a family's investable assets should be in gold or one its sister commodities.[15] Each person has to consider just how much is enough. I have always thought it a good idea to own a little and to own the coins or bullion. Again, gold is not a good investment but is the best hedge against our faceless adversaries.

CHAPTER 10

FIFTY FINANCIAL TERMS

"If you're trying to persuade people to do something or buy something, it seems to me you should use the language they use every day, the language in which they think."
—David Ogilvy

One of the greatest discourtesies any member of a profession can impose upon their respective clients or customers is to assume everyone understands their professional language. As I earlier referenced, this was my mistake when I approached the owner of the manufacturing company my first year in the business. Even the most educated among us, without the advantage of being in a particular discipline, will not necessarily appreciate the language of finances.

I can point to the medical, legal, automobile, accounting, real estate, and dozens of other professions—each with its own vernacular. To some extent I believe that financial people sometimes try to impress their audience with their intelligence by using fifty-cent words that no one else understands.

An advisor could say, "I really believe that in light of the CPI being as modest as it is, coupled with the current Fed monetary restraints, we should be cautious and diversify into alternative investments." This statement may make sense to a lot of people but certainly not everyone. The good advisor breaks the statement down in more understandable language and may say the very same thing in language common to everyone: "Because prices are not rising very quickly and because interest rates are pretty low, we might be better served by making sure your money is safe. Let's talk about how you feel about owning some investments outside of the stock market." The good advisor says the same thing only in more understandable language.

Understanding Fifty Common Phrases and Words Your Advisor Uses

Following are fifty phrases and definitions that many people have heard but maybe lack even a cursory understanding of what they mean. I really don't believe that one has to master the language. But an appreciation for these terms is important to further understanding and communicating with your advisor. Remember that an investor need not fully comprehend the many nuances of the financial industry, but to articulate your concern about a holding or a suggestion is of paramount import. Not only does it give the investor further confidence, it reminds the advisor that you are informed.

1. Adjusted gross income (AGI): AGI is a common accounting and financial term that is used in the computation of income tax liability. It's generally an interim calculation and is computed by subtracting allowable deductions from one's gross income.

2. After-tax return: Once you've sold a stock (for instance, at a profit), you will owe the IRS a capital gain tax. For example, a stock purchased for $10 and sold for $15 generates a $5 gain. This is the pretax return. The after-tax return is what you have left following payment to the government.

3. Alpha: This is the historical measure of an asset's return compared to the risk adjusted expected return. In other words, how this investment is doing relative to like investments. Do you own the best performing asset? **Beta**, in contrast, is a measure of volatility. The Standard & Poor's 500 Index is assigned a beta of 1.0 percent, so if you own an investment with a beta of, say, 1.25, you can expect your asset to be more volatile. Likewise, a beta of .80 percent will tell you that your investment is less volatile. This is an important measurement because if your mutual fund of stock has a higher beta, over time you should have better returns simply because you've had to endure a bumpy ride.

4. Alternative investments: Alternatives, or "alt investments," include venture capital (VC), private equity (nontraded ownership in a company), real estate investment trusts (REITs), and commodities such as gold, silver, pork bellies, rare coins, art, diamonds, and even wine. These investments typically do not move in tandem with the stock market and thus are called alternatives to the market. If one is right on an alternative that person stands to make a boatload; if they're wrong, they will lose a boatload.

5. Annuities: This is a contract issued by an insurance company. The contract comes with guarantees backed by the ability of the insurer to make good on its promises. If the insurer goes out of business, the annuity holder is out of his or her investment. (Only choose the highest-quality insurance company you can when making this choice.) Annuities can be either fixed or variable. **Fixed annuities** provide a predetermined amount or percentage of one's investment on a monthly, quarterly, or annual basis. Think of a CD from the bank backed by FDIC—only this investment is backed by the insurance company. **Variable annuities** are tied to an index or the market. The insurance company will place your investment in a separate account that you have chosen and then wraps a guarantee around it. For instance, you invest $100,000 in a variable annuity with a 5 percent income guarantee. If the market value of the separate account grows to $120,000, you receive 5 percent on the entire amount it has appreciated. If the market value depreciates to $80,000, you still get the benefit of receiving 5 percent on your $100,000 investment. Some companies even guarantee a certain annual growth rate, assuring you that your investment will always provide growing income to you and your family. Also, the investment will grow tax deferred, but when you access the income stream you will pay ordinary income tax. Annuities vary greatly. Make sure you understand the prospectus.

6. Asset allocation: You'll hear this one a lot. It simply means that your total investment is allocated between and among several asset classes such as large U.S. stocks, foreign stocks, bonds, treasuries, cash, and many other potential asset classes. Asset allocation does not guarantee performance, but it does base the allocation on historical data. It is intended to mitigate risk, so if a person is 100 percent invested in U.S. stocks and the market drops precipitously, the investor is perhaps better protected because he or she is diversified.

7. Basis points: Usually a ratio that is tied to fees, but it can be used to measure performance or interest rates: 100 basis points equal 1 percent. You may hear an advisor refer to basis points as bps (pronounced *bipps*.). Basis points will often be discussed when you ask your advisor about fees. He or she will tell you, "I charge 125 basis points on the value of your account." That means if you have $1 million with the advisor, you will be charged $12,500 (1.25 percent) annually.

8. Bear market: This is when the market goes down over a period of time usually by 20 percent or more. Bear markets typically occur every three-and-a-half years or so and last for about fifteen months. There have been thirty-two bear markets from 1900 through 2013.[1] A correction is when the stock market goes down about 10 percent, usually once per year. You should not fear a bear market, but be respectful of historical information. You should also make certain your exposure is appropriate for you comfort. If you can't bear (no pun intended) to watch your value go down, diversify and steer clear of stocks. One of the legends of the financial industry, Shelby Cullom Davis, founder of the Davis Funds, reminded investors, "You make most of your money in a bear market, you just don't realize it at the time."[2]

9. Blue-chip stock: Think of large, well-established companies that have been around for many years. They are typically billion-dollar companies, ones you would expect to recognize (such as Coca Cola, Disney, Intel, IBM, General Mills, etc.). These companies typically pay quarterly dividends and have for many years.

10. Book value: The net value of a company's assets minus its liabilities. If the company were to sell everything, what would be left? That's the book value, and it might be higher or lower than the stock price. As a buyer we would obviously prefer to see the book value higher than the market price.

11. Bull market: This is when the stock market goes higher over a period of time. It's the opposite of a bear market. Owners like to see the value of their stock investments go higher and enjoy the benefit of a bull market. Caution: Bull markets can be deceptive and entice people to buy into momentum. That's our greed taking over, similar to the run up in the late 1990s and 2009–2017.

12. Capital gain or loss: How much did you pay for an investment, and how much did you sell it for? If you sold it for more, you've earned a capital gain; if you sold it for less, you have a capital loss. Losses can offset gains in any calendar year, and gains will generate a "capital gains tax."

13. Collateralized mortgage obligations (CMOs): Collateralized mortgage obligations refer to a type of mortgage-backed security that contains a pool of mortgages bundled together and sold as an investment. As borrowers of home loans repay their mortgages, investors receive income, and the mortgages themselves serve as collateral. CMOs were largely responsible for the 2007–2008 financial crises.[3] The real estate market was hot, and investors thought home values would continue to go up.

But foreclosures and a general downturn in home prices caused issuers of these investments to file bankruptcy, and millions of CMO owners lost billions of dollars.

14. Commodities: Precious metals like gold and silver, livestock, grains, foodstuffs, oils. These commodities are traded on national exchanges and owned by only very well-informed investors. Do you know which direction the price of gold is going? If you anticipate a geopolitical calamity, own gold. But who has a crystal ball? Commodities will not pay a dividend.

15. Common stock: A unit of ownership in a corporation. Buy 100 shares of McDonald's and you own a piece of the giant food company. If McDonald's sales and profits go up, the value of your 100 shares should also go up. You are also entitled to quarterly dividends as an owner of common stock, assuming the company pays a dividend.

16. Dividend: Companies that provide shareholders with a dividend are able to do so because they are typically profitable and well financed. A dividend is simply a pro-rata portion of earnings and is typically distributed quarterly. Years ago when a stockbroker would recommend a company, the client would ask, "What does it pay?" It's still a good question to ask.

17. Dollar cost average: A smart way to buy stocks or mutual funds as you are not committing all your money at one time. Dollar cost averaging entails deploying a set amount of money into an investment on a regular basis: "I want to own $100,000 in a mutual fund, but I don't know if I'm buying at a high or low level. I think I'll buy $5,000 each month for the next twenty months, thus taking advantage of both high and low markets." This strategy is most appropriate for longer-term buyers.

18. Efficient frontier: You'll hear and maybe see a diagram called the efficient frontier. It employs historical data and helps an investor decide just what level of risk he or she is willing to take to receive a desired return. One might be more inclined to own a blend of U.S. stocks, foreign stocks, treasuries, foreign debt, cash, and so forth, thus minimizing volatility and risk. Armed with historical returns a person can get an idea of what type of outcome "should" be produced. History cannot anticipate every economic scenario, so consider the efficient frontier to be a model only.

19. Estate tax: When someone dies, the federal government and some states impose a tax on the deceased's estate if it is valued above a certain amount. This is a critical variable for people who have a high net worth and who intend to distribute their wealth to family, charity, or anyplace other than the government. Many wealthy people who die without a trust or even a will risk the government deciding where the assets will go. Elvis Presley, Prince, James Gandolfini, Philip Seymour Hoffman, and many others died without proper planning, and their assets were heavily taxed and definitely did not go to the beneficiaries of their choices.

20. Exchange traded funds (ETFs): The quick definition is a mutual fund that trades like a stock. Whereas a mutual fund trades at net asset value and is valued at close of market days, an ETF trades throughout the day, and prices change as shares are bought and sold. ETFs have been popularized in recent years because there are considerable price advantages to owning them. Most ETFs follow a particular index. For instance, one can buy an ETF that tracks the S&P 500 Index or the stock market in China.

21. Fixed income: Income an investor receives from CDs, Social Security, pensions, some annuities, bonds, and other investments that is the same each month. (It's fixed.)

22. Fundamental analysis: When evaluating, company analysts will employ either fundamental or technical analysis. Fundamental analysis uses factors such as price-earnings ratios, dividend yield, and return-on-equity types of reviews. It is sometimes referred to as bottom-up analysis.

23. Individual retirement accounts (IRAs): IRAs revolutionized the marketplace when they caught on in the early 1980s. Banks and brokerage companies advertised an almost-sure way to build wealth. And the fact of the matter is, IRAs are a terrific vehicle whereby workers can dollar cost average into a tax-deferred account. Contributions to a traditional IRA are deductible from earned income in the calculation of federal and state income taxes if the taxpayer meets certain income requirements. When funds are accessed (by law in the year following the worker turning seventy and six months) the income is taxed at ordinary income rates. There are also ROTH IRAs that can provide the owner with tax-deferred growth and tax-free income withdrawal and is worthy of further conversation with your advisor.

24. Inflation: Also referred to as CPI (consumer price index), inflation is any increase in the cost of goods and services. Inflation takes place when too much currency chases too few goods and services. **Deflation,** on the other hand, is a period whereby prices remain stagnant or slide lower. Japan has endured three decades of no to slow growth because of deflation. This is caused by the opposite of inflation (namely, too many goods and services and not enough money to purchase, so businesses are forced to lower prices to accommodate the consumer). During the Carter administration, inflation was in the double digits, exacerbating economic growth and undermining confidence in the overall economy. Post–First World War Germany, Argentina, Israel, Zimbabwe, and many other national economies throughout history have fallen prey to hyperinflation that wipes out wealth.

25. Insurance (term, whole life, long-term care): Nobody likes insurance, and everybody needs it. Life insurance can be divided into two broad categories: term and whole life. There are variations of both, and both have advantages. Term is so named because the insurance company is willing to pay the insured's beneficiaries a death benefit if the insured dies within the term of the policy (ten, fifteen, or twenty years). If the insured has the good fortune of surviving the term, the policy and all the premiums that were paid to own the protection are gone, and the insured has no further protection against death. (This may be very appropriate for parents with limited income but who desire the benefit of protecting their family in the event of one of the parents' deaths.) Whole life is more expensive but is permanent. The beneficiary of the insured will always have the benefit of an at-death payment. Additionally, whole life has cash value that gradually builds up and can benefit the owner during his or her lifetime. It can also be used to cover future premiums. Long-term care insurance comes into play if an older or incapacitated owner needs custodial or acute care, in a facility or even at-home care. It may constitute an important aspect of a family not spending down an estate. Long-term care insurance might very well pay for the beneficiary's assisted-living or nursing home expenses. There are many choices when it comes to providers, so be careful with your selection of term, whole life, or long-term care, as the features and benefits are widely varied. Its best to find a caring and experienced advisor who can lead you through the many options available.

26. Liability: The opposite of an asset. A company owns assets and owes liabilities, such as accounts payable, dividends declared payable, accrued taxes payable, all mortgages, bank loans, and unsecured debt.

27. Limited partnership: Limited partnerships pool the money of investors to develop or purchase income-producing real estate. Money flows through the partnership and is distributed to the shareholders. Investors need to qualify to own shares of a limited partnership and must meet the standard of accredited investor. This means that the investor has to verify that he or she has sufficient wealth and liquidity to absorb a loss. This speaks to the nature of this sometimes risky venture. Before buying, be certain to read the prospectus carefully. It may indeed be an appropriate position to own, but you need to go in with both eyes wide open. One more note: The investor does not receive a 1099 tax form, rather a K-1 form that usually arrives late and will cost you extra to have your taxes completed. K-1 forms are more complex and are subject to several last-minute amendments in an effort to remain in compliance with accounting guidelines.

28. Liquidity: Liquidity is how quickly you can get your hands on cash, or how quickly and easily you can convert an asset or security into cash. Your home is not liquid; your stocks are liquid.

29. Living will: Often referred to as an advance medical directive, a living will is used to outline which medical procedures you want to be used to prolong your life in the event of terminal illness or accident. In the absence of a living will, the hospital and doctors will do their best to sustain the patient, even if it means keeping a patient alive artificially.

30. Marital deduction: This is a provision of the federal tax code that allows all assets of a deceased spouse to pass to the surviving spouse free of estate taxes. It is referred to as the unlimited marital deduction.

31. Market capitalization: Market capitalization is the total value of the shares a company has outstanding and is calculated by multiplying the number of shares by the current market price. Here's an example: XYZ company has one hundred million shares outstanding, trading at $12 per share. XYZ's market capitalization is $1.2 billion.

32. Monte Carlo simulation: This is a mathematical model designed to understand the impact of risk and uncertainty to a portfolio of investments. It is also used in project management, cost, and insurance scenarios. It is computer generated and helps decision-makers with a range of possible outcomes. Can all probabilities be ascertained? Not in my opinion, but Monte Carlo simulation can be useful to mitigate extremes. Monte Carlo, of course, is the famous gaming resort town in Monaco. So I guess the authors of this process also say it as a bit of a gamble.

33. Municipal bonds: This is a debt security issued by municipalities and states. The chief advantage of owning municipal bonds (munis) is federal tax-free income. If the bond owner resides in the state where the bond was issued, he or she may also receive interest, free of state income taxes. Municipals are graded relative to their credit worthiness. Highly considered bonds might be rated AAA or AA and may carry insurance. Other bonds may not be as safe and will have a *B* or *C* rating, and for the risk an investor takes, it will pay a higher interest. Municipal bonds can be sold in lots of $10,000 or may be contained in a mutual fund. In a fund there will be several different bonds varying in quality and maturity, and the fund will be managed by a professional. The result is the same. Interest will be delivered tax free. It is important to note that a bondholder who sells the bond prior to maturity may get more or less than the investment. Bonds trade relative to prevailing interest rates.

34. Mutual funds: A collection of stocks, bonds, or other securities purchased and professionally managed by an investment company. The return and principal values of mutual funds fluctuate with changes in the overall markets. Mutual funds are sold by prospectus and describe all costs and objectives. Mutual funds have been highly popular during the past several decades and are typically ideal for people who have a need for professional management. Fund families such as Vanguard, Fidelity, American, MFS, First Eagle, and thousands of others usually offer a wide variety of investment options for a wide variety of personal objectives.

35. Net asset value (NAV): The per-share value of a mutual fund's current holdings. The net asset value is calculated at the close of markets each day and is determined by dividing the net market value of the fund's holdings by the number of shares in the fund.

36. Portfolio: All the investments owned by an individual or family. A couple in their eighties should have a significantly different portfolio than a couple in their thirties. This is an important variable to understand. (The older couple should have more bonds and cash, as they have relatively less time to recover from a down market.)

37. Preferred stock: A class of stock that is senior to common stock. Preferreds receive preferential treatment if the company is forced to liquidate. This type of stock also pays a fixed dividend that is considered safer than common stock dividends.

38. Price-to-earnings ratio (P/E ratio): The market price of the stock divided by the company's annual earnings per share. Earnings are critical to companies, so if a stock price is trading low relative to the company's earnings, it is typically more desirable to own. Think of a Blue Light Special at Kmart! The company may be on sale. Also, prognosticators like to predict future earnings, so they will point to next quarter's or next year's P/E ratio. They may be right, but they are certainly using a degree of conjecture.

39. Prospectus: A legal and important document provided by investment companies to investors. The prospectus gives information needed by investors to make intelligent decisions prior to buying shares in a mutual fund, variable annuity, variable universal life insurance, or limited partnership. Contained in the prospectus are fund objectives, expenses, past performance, risk levels, and sales charges. Nobody likes to read the legalese of a prospectus, but each investment should be strongly considered by reading the prospectus prior to buying.

40. Real estate investment trusts (REITs): Companies that own, and in most cases operate, income-producing real estate. REITS may own commercial real estate such as office buildings and apartment buildings, warehouses, hospitals, shopping centers, and even hotels. Think of a REIT as a mutual fund for people who want to own real estate.

41. Retirement plan: When you hear 401(k), 403(b), pension, IRA, SIMPLE, SEP-IRA, and so on, someone is talking about a retirement plan. I believe the operative word is "plan." Many people who don't have a formal retirement plan enact their own. This might include an annuity, tax deferred account, or simply a large savings position with little or no debt. Social Security has been called a retirement vehicle. Very few people can subsist on Social Security alone. The best retirement plan includes Social Security, savings, tax-deferred accumulation, and quality investments with little or no debt. Americans who successfully plan have a fighting chance to live comfortably in retirement.

42. Revocable living trust (RLT): A legal document in which the creator reserves the right to modify or terminate the trust. RLTs are highly popular among people who are growing wealth and have a need for more comprehensive estate planning. Revocable living trusts often include living wills and medical directives as well as reciprocal powers of attorneys. The creator(s) can also be very specific regarding distribution of assets. There are no estate tax advantages to adopting an RLT.

43. Risk: The chance that an investor will lose all or part of an investment. Even though U.S. treasuries are referred to as "riskless" investments, every investment contains risk, including treasuries and cash.

44. Step up in basis: When a person who bought a stock or mutual fund (or property) dies, the price he or she paid for the investment "steps up" to the person's date of death, thus benefiting the recipient of the property. There are important exceptions to this, and I encourage the reader to get current information (IRS.gov is a good source.)

45. Tax credit: A very appealing tax advantage and a lot better than a deduction. Tax credits are subtracted dollar for dollar from your bottom line income tax bill. If you have a $5,000 tax credit and your tax bill was $10,000, you would owe only $5,000.

46. Tax deferred: Literally deferring taxes until income is withdrawn. Your money grows tax free until you choose to access the income. At that point, tax is imposed.

47. Technical analysis: This is quite different from fundamental analysis. This is an approach to investing in stocks in which a stock's past performance is mapped onto charts. The technical analyst is looking for patterns to use as an indicator of the stock's future.

48. Total return: The total of all earnings from any investment including dividends, interest, and capital gain.

49. Volatility: The complete range of price swings over a period of time. One might refer to the Dow Jones as being volatile, meaning wide swings in price. The VIX is an index of volatility that helps determine just how volatile the market has been.

50. Yield: This is what percentage of income either dividends or interest a security is paying. Dividend-paying stocks pay a percentage of earnings to shareholders, usually quarterly. Bond issuers pay a stated percentage of interest to owners, usually twice per year. Yield should never be confused with total return.

FINAL NOTE

No one knows what the future may bring, and my admonition to the reader is be vigilant with your resources beginning with your personal protection and extending it to the Madoffs among us.

Ecclesiastes 1:9 reminds us that "what has been will be again, what has been done will be done again, there is nothing new thing under the sun." I truly believe that from the time Satan tempted the naïve Eve with his subtlety until the present and beyond, we will always be susceptible to the twin towers of deceit: subtlety and naïveté.

Caveat emptor, my friend!

ACKNOWLEDGMENTS

An author's name may be on the cover, but it is often-times the people behind the book that deserve the most credit.

Judy Cohen, who became my friend, held me accountable to finish this important work. Deb Englander told me, "This work deserves a publisher" and encouraged me to seek out the best I could find. Martha Bullen served as my guiding light, asking tough questions and keeping me on task. Raia King steered me in the right direction relative to marketing as her baby girl, Alex, cooed in the background during conference calls. Steve Harrison put together a remarkable menu of services designed to help a fledgling author. Geoffrey Berwin took me under his wing and guided my enthusiasm for my message.

When I met John Willig, he saw my vision, believed in me, and fortunately became my literary agent. He intro-duced me to Red Wheel, Michael Pye, Laurie Pye, Lauren Manoy, Jodi Brandon, Gina Schenck, Tess Woods, and the staff of consummate professionals who agreed to take a chance on a first-time author.

I also want to acknowledge the talent of Jessica Francavilla and Shari Gann for helping to present a clear and concise marketing message on social media.

Special thanks to my esteemed colleagues who agreed to read the manuscript and offer valuable and constructive advice, including Raymond "Chip" Mason, Pat Socci, Kathleen Hebbeler, Tim Scheve, Rick Myers, Gerri Leder, and Mike Whittaker. Julie Anne Lewis and Gary D. Bonnewell played special roles with their enthusiastic support and industry expertise. And a heartfelt thanks to Jim Brinkley, for agreeing to write the foreword and for his personal encouragement to tell the story.

I'm sure there are many more people I should thank but no one—repeat, no one—is more deserving of my gratitude than my wife, Rita, who not only puts up with my delusions of grandeur but serves as my most severe and loving critic. Her artistic abilities, intelligence, and honest opinions of everything I wrote is the reason *The Madoffs Among Us* is everything I envisioned.

NOTES

Chapter 1

1. Laura Hensley, "It Was All Gone: Former NHLer Bryan Berard Explains How Fraudsters Devastated His Retirement Savings," *National Post* (Toronto, Ontario), July 15, 2015.
2. Ibid.
3. Ibid.
4. Certified Financial Planner Board of Standards, "Senior Financial Exploitation Study," Certified Financial Planner Board of Standards website, August 2012, *www.cfp.net/docs/news-events---supporting-documents/senior-americans-financial-exploitation-survey.pdf?sfvrsn=0*.
5. Paul Grein, "Billy Joel Sues Former Manager for $90 Million," *Los Angeles Times,* September 26, 1989.
6. Philip Boroff, "What Art Collectors Can Learn from Art Thief Larry Salander," *Barron's,* May 16, 2015.
7. Mary Braid, "Sting's Advisor Jailed for Pounds 6M Theft from Star," *The Independent* (London), October 17, 1995.
8. Mark Egan, Gregor Matvos, and Amit Seru, "The Market for Financial Advisor Misconduct," February 29, 2016, *papers.ssrn.com.*
9. Anna Prior, "Brokers Are Trusted Less than Uber Drivers, Survey Finds," *The Wall Street Journal,* July 28, 2015.

Chapter 2

1. Information in this chapter, unless specifically noted, was culled from a variety of sources: "Bernard Madoff," *en.wikipedia.org/wiki/Bernard_madoff*; "Bernie Madoff," *www.investopedia.com/terms/b/bernard-madoff.asp?ad=dirN&qo=investopediaSiteSearch&qsrc=0&o=40186*; Stephanie Yang, "5 Years Ago Bernie Madoff Was Sentenced to 150 Years in Prison—Here's How His Scheme Worked," *Business Insider,* July 1, 2014, *www.businessinsider.com/how-bernie-madoffs-ponzi-scheme-worked-2014-7*; "Charles Ponzi," *en.wikipedia.org?charles_ponzi*; "Charles Ponzi," *www.u-s-history.com/pages/h1800*; "Mississippi Company," *en.wikipedia.org/wiki/Mississippi_company*; Jon Moen, "John Law and the Mississippi Bubble 1718–1720," *www.mshistorynow.mdah.ms.gov/articles/70/john-law-and-the-mississippi-bubble-1718-1720*; "John Law (Economist)", *en.wikipedia.org/wiki/John_Law_(economist)*; "Kenneth Lay," *en.wikipedia.org/wiki/Kenneth_lay*; "Kenneth Lay," *www.biography.com/people/kenneth-lay-234611*; "Bernard Ebbers," *en.wikipedia.org/wiki/Bernard_Ebbers*; "Bernard Ebbers," *www.biography.com/people/bernard-ebbers-233081*.

2. Randall Smith, "Wall St. Mystery Features a Big Board Rival," *The Wall Street Journal,* December 16, 1992.

3. "S&P 500 Annual Return," *https://ycharts.com/indicators/sandp_500_return_annual*.

4. Kara Scannell, "Madoff Chasers Dug for Years to No Avail," *The Wall Street Journal,* January 5, 2009.

5. Reuven Fenton, "Bernie Madoff Sentenced to 150 Years in Prison," *The New York Post,* June 29, 2009.

6. Dan Strumpf, "Madoff Scandal Still Haunts Victims," *The Wall Street Journal,* December 10, 2012.

7. Cheryl Isaac, "Ruth Madoff in Her 60 Minutes Interview: 'Whether I Would Have Turned Him in or Not, I Can't Say'," *Forbes,* October 31, 2011.

8. Lionel S. Lewis, *Con Game: Bernard Madoff and His Victims* (Routledge, 2012).

9. Mary Darby, "In Ponzi We Trust," December 1998, *Smithsonian.com*.

10. Ibid.
11. Herbert Baldwin, "Canadian Ponzi Served Jail Time," *Boston Post,* August 11, 1920.
12. Darby, "In Ponzi We Trust."
13. Charles Mackey, *Extraordinary Popular Delusions and the Madness of Crowds* (Wordsworth Edition Ltd., 1984).
14. Robert Linzer, "Thomas Jefferson Warned the Nation to Beware the Power of Banks," *Forbes,* November 6, 2011.
15. Stephen M. Bainbridge, *The Complete Guide to Sarbanes Oxley: Understanding How Sarbanes Oxley Works* (New York: Simon & Schuster, 2007).
16. Judith Yates, *How to Recognize the Devil: Common Sense Self Defense & Crime Prevention Handbook* (J.A. Yates, 2014).
17. Simon Lovell, *How to Cheat at Everything: A Con Man Reveals the Secrets of the Esoteric Trade of Cheating, Scams, and Hustles* (Philadelphia: Running Press, 2007).

Chapter 3

1. *SEC, Plaintiff v. Michael Donnelly, Defendant,* Civil Action No. 15-5873, Department of Justice, U.S. Attorney's Office, Eastern District of Pennsylvania, April 11, 2016
2. United States of America before the Securities and Exchange Commission, May 9, 2014
3. Department of Justice, U.S. Attorney's Office, District of Minnesota, March 1, 2016; "Advisor Pleads Guilty to Stealing from Clients in Minnesota and Wisconsin," *justice.gov.*
4. Ibid.
5. A life insurance annuity may have both cash value and investment value. An owner can redeem an annuity providing investable funds, and an advisor can generate a commission by redeploying the assets.
6. U.S. Attorney's Office, District of Nevada, February 11, 2014, *brokercheck.finra.org.*
7. "Nate Raymond Investment Advisor Imprisoned for Fraud Tied to Kickbacks, Horse Racing," Reuters, February 13, 2015.
8. Ibid.; Department of Justice, U.S. Attorney's Office, Southern District of New York, February 13, 2015.

9. "Former Broker at San Fernando Valley Brokerage Firm Sentenced to 18 Months in Federal Prison for Defrauding Investors," Department of Justice, U.S. Attorney's Office, Central District of California, October 19, 2015, press release #15-110.

10. John Nickson, "Former Darien Broker Pleads Guilty to Stealing $1.2 Million," *Stamford Advocate* (Connecticut), June 17, 2016; Department of Justice, U.S. Attorney's Office, District of Connecticut, October 5, 2016.

11. Trevor Hunicutt, "Advisor Faces Nine Years in Prison for Diverting Investment Funds," *Investment News,* May 18, 2015.

12. Ibid.

13. U.S. Attorney's Office, District of Minnesota, June 26, 2015.

14. Jeff Manning, "Five Months Since Collapse, Aequitas Investors Go on Attack," *The Oregonian/Oregon Live,* January 26, 2017.

15. Ibid.; U.S. District Court, District of Oregon, Portland, March 10, 2016.

16. Mihir A. Desai, "Financial Fraud: It Takes Two," *The Atlantic,* August 9, 2017.

Chapter 4

1. "FINRA Foundation Survey Reveals Over 80% of Respondents Are Exposed to Financial Scams," FINRA Investor Education Foundation.

2. Martha Deevy and Michaela Beals, "The Scope of the Problem," Stanford Center on Longevity/FINRA, 2013.

3. Karla Pak and Doug Shadel, "AARP Foundation National Fraud Victim Study," Research & Strategic Analysis, 2011.

4. "Baby Boomers to Retire," PEW Research Center, December 29, 2010.

5. Carolyn Yoon, Catherine Cole, and Michelle Lee, "Decision Making and Aging," *ink.library.smu.edu/sg/cgi.*

6. Lovell, *How to Cheat at Everything.*

7. This includes several resources adding up to much more than $100 billion, for example: Haydn Shaughnessy, "Solving the $190 Billion Annual Fraud Problem," *Forbes,* March 24, 2011; Henry McDonald, "Online Fraud Costs Global Economy

'Many Times More than $100 Billion,'" *The Guardian,* October 30, 2013; and "Medicare Fraud: A $60 Billion Crime," *CBS News,* October 23, 2009.

Chapter 5

1. Sid Kirchheimer, "Busted: Con Artists Exposed," *AARP Bulletin,* January–February 2014.
2. Ibid.
3. Information and quotes in this section are from David Moye, "Tracy Vasseur, Karen Vasseut Sentenced to Jail for 'Nigerian Internet Romance Scam,'" *Huffington Post,* August 30, 2013.
4. Information and quotes in this section are from Jeb Phillips, "Scammers Pretend to Be Veterans Charities," *Columbus Dispatch* (Ohio), June 23, 2013.
5. Information in this section is from "Canadian Man Pleads Guilty to Scamming Grandmothers," CBS/AP, Bangor Maine, June 12, 2012.
6. Information and quotations in this section are from Kelly Gardner, "10 Busted in Statewide Sting Targeting Those Who Con Elderly," *WRAL.com,* Raleigh, North Carolina, July 29, 2013.
7. Information and quotations in this section are from Peter Hall, "State Attorney General Announces Charges in Widespread Senior Scam," *Morning Call* (Lehigh County, Pennsylvania), May 22, 2012.
8. Information and quotations in this section are from "More Prison Time for Former Investment Advisor," DOJ, U.S. Attorney's Office, District of Massachusetts, August 7, 2015.
9. Information and quotations in this section are from Robert Patrick and Susan Weich, "Controversial St. Charles Pastor Admits Defrauding Elderly Investors," *St. Louis Post-Dispatch,* April 30, 2015.
10. Adam Brownlee, January 21, 2016, Investopedia website, *investopedia.com.*
11. Pamela Yellen, "Dalbar 2014 QAIB Report Reveals the Truth About Investor Returns," April 30, 2014, *bankonyourself.com.*
12. Ibid.

13. Ashna Kumar Thane, "Mumbai: Cops Arrest Kingpin Sagar Thakkar Alias 'Shaggy' for Duping Americans," *India Today*, April 8, 2017.

Chapter 6

1. See *data.worldbank.org*.
2. John Fleming, "Gallup Analysis: Millennials, Marriage and Family," May 19, 2016, *news.gallup.com*.
3. Chloe Della Costa, "9 Medical Procedure that Cost Way Too Much," *USA Today*, March 28, 2015.
4. Pool are considered attractive nuisances in the insurance industry, and dogs (oftentimes depending on breed and training) can be unpredictable. Approximately four-and-a-half million dog bites occur each year in the United States (*www.law.cornell.edu/wex/attractive_nuisance_doctrine; www.cdc.gov/feature s/dog-bite-prevention/index*).
5. Maria LaMagna, "Americans Now Have the Highest Credit Card Debt in U.S. History," *Market Watch*, August 8, 2017.
6. Ibid.
7. Seth Meyers, "How Financial Problems and Stress Cause Divorce," *psychologytoday.com*.
8. Kelly Phillips Erb, "Raking it in at Summer Yard Sales: Does Uncle Sam Get a Cut?" *Forbes*, June 22, 2014.
9. "The 5 Deadly Sins of Investing," *ThinkAdvisor*, August 16, 2016.
10. "Market Volatility: A Guide to Riding the Waves," Morningstar website, *morningstar.com/elabslinks/volatilitypacket2015*.
11. Paul R. La Monica, "Bill Miller's Streak Strikes Out: For the First Time in 15 Years, the Legendary Fund Manager's Legg Mason Value Trust Won't Bea the S&P 500," *CNN Money*, December 29, 2016.
12. Kimberly Amadeo, "National Debt by Year Compared to GDP and Major Events," *The Balance*, updated November 7, 2017.
13. Rob Stein, "Life Expectancy in U.S. Drops for First Time in Decades, Report Finds," NPR Radio IQ, December 8, 2016.
14. Eric Pianin, "10,000 Boomers Turn 65 Every Day. Can Medicare and Social Security Handle It?" *The Fiscal Times*, May 9, 2017.

15. "2016 Retirement Preparedness Survey Findings," Perspectives on Retirement, *research.prudential.com.*

Chapter 7

1. "A Mean Feat," *The Economist,* January 9, 2016.
2. Joel Anderson, "The Best Quotes of Benjamin Graham," February 16, 2012, *equities.com.*
3. Steven Goldberg, "Make Money in a Bear Market," *Kiplinger,* December 4, 2007.
4. Nate Silver, *The Signal and the Noise: Why So Many Predictions Fail—But Some Don't* (New York: Penguin Books, 2015).
5. Alexander Jung, "Germany in the Era of Hyperinflation," *Spiegel* online, August 14, 2009.
6. Brian Taylor, "The Death of the Zimbabwe Dollar," Global Financial Data, undated.
7. "The Tragedy of Argentina: A Century of Decline," *The Economist,* February 17, 2014.
8. Philip Wegmann, "America's Real Debt Shocker: $100 Trillion Owed in Unfunded Liabilities," *The National Interest,* June 14, 2016.
9. Cardiff Garcia, "Deflationary Periods in US History," Chart: CPI Inflation (1882–1938 Annual Rates), *Financial Times,* October 6, 2010.
10. Barry Nielsen, "The Lost Decade: Lessons from Japan's Real Estate Crisis," Investopedia website, *www.investopedia.com/articles/economics/08/japan-1990s-credit-crunch-liquidity-trap.asp?lgl=myfinance-layout-no-ads.*
11. Kevin Pollard and Paola Scommegna, April 2014, Population Reference Bureau website, prb.org.
12. William Power, "9/17/01: Wall Street's Proudest Day. A Look Back on the Reopening," *Wall Street Journal,* September 5, 2016.
13. "Bear Markets and Economic Contractions: 2001/2008," Ciovacco Capital Management, LLC website, *http://ciovaccocapital.com/wordpress/index.php/stock-market-us/bear-markets-and-economic-contractions-20012008-vs-2015/.*
14. Joseph E. Stiglitz, "The True Cost of 9/11," *Slate,* September 1, 2011.

15. "The Experts: Should the Average American Buy Gold?" *Wall Street Journal*, May 7, 2013.

Chapter 8
1. "Rule 405," *https://financial-dictionary.thefreedictionary.com /Rule+405*.
2. Ibid.
3. Bernice Napach, "The Real Cost of Investment Fees," *ThinkAdvisor*, September 13, 2015.
4. Brian O'Connell, "Red Flags that Could Mean Leaving Your Financial Advisor," *The Street,* September 22, 2015.

Chapter 9
1. Lauren Lyster, "Jim Rogers Fund Made 4,200% While the S&P 500 Only Returned 47%," February 3, 2013, *valuewalk .com/2016/08/jim-rogers-returns/*.
2. "Standard & Poor's 500 Index History Chart, January 4, 1960 through December 30, 2016," *fedprimerate.com*.
3. Miranda Marquit, "What's the Difference Between a RIA and a Broker Dealer?" updated September 29, 2017, *investorjunkie .com*.
4. See *finra.org/investors/about-brokercheck-reports*.

Glossary
1. Tim Mullaney, "8 Things You Need to Know about Bear Markets," August 24, 2015, *cnbc.com/2015/08*.
2. Larissa Fernand, "The Time to Make Money Is in a Bear Market," Morningstar, May 13, 2016.
3. "Were Collateralized Mortgage Obligations (CMOs) Responsible for the Financial Crisis of 2008?" Investopedia, October 26, 2017.

INDEX

B shares, 114

Bacon, Kevin, Bernie Madoff and, 35

Banco Zarossi, Carlo Ponzi and, 40

Barron, Clarence, Carlo Ponzi and, 43

basis points, 189

bear market, 189

Belfort, Jordan, 83

Berard, Bryan, 15-16, 21-22, 27

Bernie Madoff, Jack Cutter and, 37

beta, an asset's return of, 187

Better Business Bureau, 80

    reputable firms through, 89-90

Binkholder, Bryan, 64-65

blue-chip stock, 189-190

Boesky, Ivan, 52

book value, 190

Boroff, Philip, 25

Brinkley, Jim, 44-45

British Petroleum, 161

broker dealer, 127-128

budget, debt reduction and, 154-158

bull market, 190

Bush, George W., Kenneth Lay and, 49

buying habits,

    fear and, 76

    greed and, 76

C shares, 114

Canadian Warehousing, Carlo Ponzi and, 40-41

capital gain, 190

capital loss, 190

    maximizing, 146

    time horizons for, 109

cash management, 108

cash reserves,

    minimum level of, 140-141

    the importance of, 138-145

cash-value insurance policies, 146

cash,

    definition of, 138

    security and, 139

    the importance of, 143-144

certifications, proper advisor, 107

Certified Financial Planner,

    job of a, 129-130

    the role of a, 107-108

Certified Fund Specialist, job of a, 130-131

Certified Investment Analyst, job of a, 131-132

Certified Planner Board of Standards, 22-23

Certified Public Accountant, job of a, 132

charging for services, advisors and, 111-116

charitable inclinations, questions about your, 104

charities, fraud through, 87-88

Chartered Financial Analyst, job of a, 130

Chartered Financial Consultant, job of a, 131

Chartered Investment Counselor, job of a, 131

Chartered Life Underwriter, job of a, 132-133

Chartered Market Technician, job of a, 132

Cherry, Bruce H., 90-91

children,

    life insurance for, 148

    questions about your, 104

collateralized mortgage obligations, 190-191

commodities, 191

common sense, fraud and using, 75

common stock, 191

Community Reinvestment Act, 145

Company d'Occident, 46

Constantine, Tommy, 22

consumer response, visceral influences and the, 77

consumers, cost of scams on, 77

contractor-licensing bureau, following up with the, 80

ABOUT THE AUTHOR

My thirty-year professional career has been in financial services. I started as a trainee with a well-respected Wall Street firm in 1986. My career included successful financial advisory with more than $400 million under personal management. As my sales career advanced, I was selected to assume responsibilities as branch manager and regional sales manager. I later was chosen to be chair of the company's branch advisory council. In 2004 I was asked to serve Legg Mason in the capacity of senior vice president, director of wealth management. My responsibilities included directing the efforts of two dozen attorneys and CPAs as we assisted high-net-worth individuals and families with sophisticated financial matters. Understanding the business from the ground up has been truly enlightening and has provided a unique perspective regarding fair versus unfair.

I have continued my formal education and in 2000 successfully completed my Certified Financial Planner® designation from the College of Financial Planning in Denver, Colorado. I also maintain a chartered financial consultant designation from the American College in Bryn Mawr, Pennsylvania. My undergraduate degree from the University of Dayton is in psychology. I have always believed that this foundational education has helped me to better understand people and has helped me in my successful career. Postgraduate education took place at both the University of Virginia and the Wharton School of the University of Pennsylvania.

Having interviewed, hired, and trained literally thousands of men and women in the industry, I believe I have a unique perspective regarding those who succeed professionally and conduct themselves in exemplary fashion always on the behalf of their clients. Unfortunately, I have met (and yes, hired) some people who are far less desirable and disappointed (or outright stolen from) their friends and clients.

As an accomplished platform speaker, I readily seek opportunities whereby I can deliver a message to investment professionals that will inspire them to do what is always in the clients' best interest. My seminars on client-focused investments have always proved to be popular. I now want to reach beyond the investment professional community and bring my message to the people most in need, the consumers. Presently, I consult with successful financial advisors across the United States. and Canada, advising them on how best to grow their practices, always with an eye on what's best for the client.